Build a
Model Railway Layout

BUILD A MODEL RAILWAY LAYOUT

Dave Lowery

ARGUS BOOKS

Argus Books
Argus House
Boundary Way
Hemel Hempstead
Hertfordshire HP2 7ST
England

First published by Argus Books 1990

ISBN 1 85486 045 3

Phototypesetting by The Works, Exeter, Devon. EX4 3LS, England.
Printed and bound in Great Britain by Dotesios Printers Ltd, Trowbridge, Wilts.

CONTENTS

Acknowledgements

Foreword

CHAPTER 1   Introduction   9

CHAPTER 2   Why a baseboard?   11

CHAPTER 3   Which scale or gauge?   14

CHAPTER 4   What's available?   20

CHAPTER 5   Design your layout first   24

CHAPTER 6   The plan   28

CHAPTER 7   Materials and tools   32

CHAPTER 8   Construction   36

CHAPTER 9   Permanent way   49

CHAPTER 10   Wiring up   59

CHAPTER 11   Electrics explained   65

CHAPTER 12   Scenics   71

CHAPTER 13   Architecture   88

CHAPTER 14   Stock   98

CHAPTER 15   Modelling tips   104

CHAPTER 16   Getting nearer the prototype   111

CHAPTER 17   Instant model railway   117

CHAPTER 18   The completed railway system   119

APPENDIX A   Manufacturers' and suppliers' addresses   121

APPENDIX B   Glossary   123

INDEX   127

DEDICATION

To Mum and Dad, with many thanks.

ACKNOWLEDGEMENTS

My thanks go to Hornby Model Railways, in particular Simon Kohlar, for supplying a large number of the items used in building this layout from their extensive range of model railway equipment; Tony Osborn, the proprietor of Model Images, who kindly supplied the rest of the items used in this project; Alan Maynard for the buildings in the town, Samantha for typing the manuscript; Peter Holland for the sketches, and Stewart Hine for the 'explaining electrics' notes.

FOREWORD

9.75 + 95p p

This book will enable you to build the layout featured on the cover. It gives all measurements and manufacturers' addresses, including the equipment used. A full-size plan is available from Argus Plans to accompany the book, and this contains all the necessary part numbers of Hornby track and wood measurements etc. – all you need to build a replica! Of course, you can put in your own modifications to our basic plan. Either way, when you've finished this book you'll have a comprehensive model railway layout.

Photos of each end of the finished layout showing two of the main areas depicted. *Above:* the loco shed (an ex-Hornby model) which can hold up to three main line locos. *Below:* the town scene, this time made up from Hornby Railways semi-detached Victorian houses and shops. In the background is the overall roof and station — an imposing structure.

1 INTRODUCTION

There have been many books over the years on the subject of getting started in model railways, and to say they are similar is an understatement. So what makes this one different? The answer is that it has a central theme which is a practical exercise, and with this book you can actually build the layout featured on the front cover – or any number of similar layouts of your own design.

As I built the layout, I photographed the different stages of progress and, as you read the chapters on baseboards, track laying, scenics, electrics, etc., I will expand on them showing a sample of the alternatives available, and clearly explaining the particular methods used in the project. This way, the newcomer, who may not wish to copy the layout blow-for-blow, can implement alternative methods in his or her project layout, or use the special plan available from our Plans Service (see Appendix A). This plan not only gives you all the Hornby track part numbers which this layout uses, but also indicates the framework for the baseboard so, should you wish to construct an identical layout, then you can take measurements directly from the plan.

The attraction of model railways is that the hobby appeals to all ages, from small children, dads encouraged by the slightest glimmer of interest from their newly born son or daughter, right up to the established expert who has been modelling for so long he's grown his own 'rivets'.

Although the steam engines of the past are only rarely seen on special outings or on preserved lines, they are still present as the impression of a train when today's children are asked to draw a railway picture. However, modern image modellers and today's youth, who live in a diesel and electric environment, are also well catered for by the hobby.

If you're a newcomer to the hobby, then your first thoughts are 'How do I start, where do I get all the information, and, most importantly, how much will it cost?' Before I answer these questions, a word of advice. Throughout the country every year there are numerous exhibitions, some connected solely with model railways, some only partially. Whichever you choose, I would strongly recommend that you attend several of these, or one of the bigger, more established shows. To find out about these exhibitions, there are several railway modelling magazines available each month. *Model Railways* gives a list of all the exhibitions and shows for a particular month, and you can select the one nearest to you that you might like to attend. Another good idea is to contact your local model railway club, which is usually registered with the local library.

Having now established the sort of modelling that you think is going to satisfy your needs, we can look at how to get started. As there are many different scales and gauges on offer, the space you have available to build a layout will probably govern your choice.

2 WHY A BASEBOARD?

The single most important necessity for model railway loco-motives and stock is to keep them clean, well maintained and, particularly, free from fluff. It never ceases to amaze me just how fluff manages to accumulate into engine mechanisms. This causes clogging of the wheels, gears and axles and removes the oil important for smooth running. So how do we get round this?

This set-up should be avoided at all costs. *Do not* lay a train set out on the lounge carpet — it will cause no end of problems.

The solution is to make a permanent base or baseboard, usually consisting of a softwood framework with a suitable covering. This can be ply, chipboard or Sundeala. This last covering is available from most specialist model railway shops and is an ideal surface. Its advantage over, say, chipboard is that it is lighter, but will require more cross-braces of softwood than chipboard since it will sag over a longer length. This will result in undulating trackwork, which we do not want.

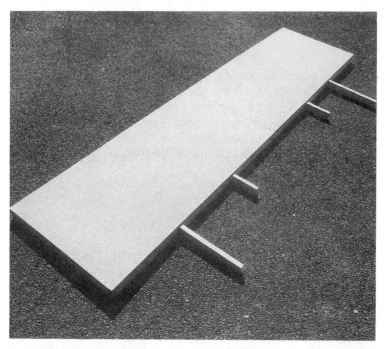

A simple baseboard can be constructed from a 2 × 1 in. softwood framework with a suitable flat covering; in this case Sundeala was used as the surface. The protruding cross-braces are to support a shaped baseboard front.

As well as keeping the layout free from dirt, a firm base allows easy transport once the trackwork is fixed, so it can easily be stored or taken to other venues, for example an exhibition. Storage is all-important. Because of their nature model railways tend to take up a large amount of space. So, once you have finished with it after an operating session (a term used by the bigger kids among us — really we're all just playing), you can store it so that normal household life can resume. Storage can be under a bed (ideally on a baseboard fitted with castors), folded up against a wall or, as I once saw in a house, actually slung from the ceiling by pulleys and ropes, pulled up out of the way when not in use — most ingenious!

The design I have chosen allows the baseboard to be free-standing, with its own legs that will fold up underneath when not in use, and the layout can be stored on its side against a wall. A simple system of folding cross-stays on the legs allows easy setting up, especially useful for one-man operation. Then put on the stock, plug in the transformer and off we go.

The finished baseboard for our project is self-supported and shows the extended shaped front and upper level which will be the terminus.

So, as you can see, a baseboard is the first basic requirement for a model railway.

3 WHICH SCALE OR GAUGE?

The selection of the most suitable scale and gauge for your model railway is always a compromise between conflicting factors. As well as being one of the first decisions to make, it is also one of the most important. Don't worry if you choose wrongly, changing scale is easy. There is plenty of scope in both stock, track and accessories, both second-hand and new, on offer to the budding modeller.

To give some idea of the size of the different scales, shown here are three coaches in N-gauge (*smallest*), 00/H0 (*centre*) and 0-gauge (*back*).

If, like most of us, you become absorbed in this very special hobby, you'll probably end up with layouts in a number of different scales and gauges, and they are likely to depict different periods and types of stock. For example, I started in 00 Hornby, or Tri-ang as it then was, and then moved into fine scale modelling over a number of years, ending up modelling to P4 standards (more on this later) the old Premier Line, the London and North Western Railway (LNWR). I've recently started in '0' gauge, this time modelling the current Modern Image scene, ie. the West Coast Main Line Electrics. I also have interests in Z-gauge American from Marklin and Kadee, and then there's this project which will be 00, 1960s steam, so you can see that, once the 'bug' has bitten, then it's only a matter of time before you get involved in several scales and gauges.

First of all, it is necessary to define clearly the terms 'gauge' and 'scale', which are often confused. *Gauge* is the distance between the inside faces of the running rails; *scale* is the factor relating dimension on the prototype to its equivalent on the model. The gauge is, of course, a prototype dimension — at least to begin with — and so the two are related; but not as simply as one might think.

The 'standard gauge', 4ft 8½in (1435mm), began as an attempt to standardize the gauges of a host of existing colliery tramways; hence the very un-round figure.

A simple table listing only the major scales and gauges may help make things clearer.

Common Name	Scale	Gauge	Ratio
Gauge 1	10mm/ft	44.45mm	1/32
'0' Gauge	7mm/ft	32mm	1/43
*00 }	4mm/ft	16.5mm	1/76
*H0 }	3.5mm/ft	16.5mm	1/87
TT	3mm/ft	12mm	1/120
N	2mm/ft	9mm	1/160 European or 1/148 British
Z	–	6.5mm	1/220

* Note, because of the common track gauge (16.5mm) these two are bracketed together, thus we have 00/H0.

The various popular gauges in actual size from Gauge 1 to Z-gauge.

We can now expand those various scales a little further as follows:

GAUGE 1

Gauge 1 was once considered the smallest practical gauge for a model railway, but is now nearly the biggest. The gauge is

1¾in (44.5mm) and the scale most commonly used is 10mm/ft; some modellers prefer ⅜in/ft (1/32) which gives a more accurate gauge/scale ratio and makes scaling from prototype drawings easier. Most Gauge 1 layouts are out-of-doors and require a larger than average garden; ready-to-run models are very expensive and even the materials for scratchbuilding cost quite a lot, due to the sheer size. The advantages of the large scale lie in the closeness of the model's behaviour to the prototype; their mass gives realistic coasting and feeling of 'real railway' operation. It is the smallest scale in which reliable live-steam locos can be built, without exceptional skill or facilities.

GAUGE 0

Gauge 0 is 32mm between the rails and the usual scale is 7mm/ft. The scale shares the advantages of Gauge 1 to a limited extent, but can be accommodated in small gardens or large lofts. Not much ready-made equipment is available but the range of kits and parts is good.

00 GAUGE

00 Gauge is 16.5mm between rails but, due to the early problems in making motors small enough to fit into the restricted British loading gauge, a compromise scale of 4mm/ft was adopted. This is the most widely used scale/gauge combination in the UK and an enormous range of ready-to-run models and kits is available.

EM AND SCALEFOUR

EM Gauge and Protofour/Scalefour represent attempts to improve the scale/gauge ratio while taking advantage of the otherwise excellent models and kits at the upper end of the 00 gauge market. EM is 18.2mm between rails; S4 and P4, with a gauge of 18.83mm, have proved that reliable running can be obtained with almost exact-scale wheel standards, given reasonable care. The relevant societies provide the necessary parts for conversion and there is some support from the commercial kit market.

H0 GAUGE

H0 Gauge is literally 'Half 0' with a gauge of 16.5mm and a scale of 3.5mm/ft. It is standard on the Continent and in America, but is seldom used for models of British prototype.

TT GAUGE

TT Gauge (standing for 'Table Top') originated in the USA with a track gauge of 12mm and scale of 1/120, giving an excellent scale/gauge ratio and allowing a layout in less space than H0. British TT was introduced by Tri-ang to 3mm/ft scale; it proved a commercial failure, but the scale of 3mm/ft (or ¼mm:1in) proved excellent for the British modeller, and there is a flourishing 3mm Society and a buoyant market in secondhand Tri-ang TT items which enable a modeller with some building ability to produce layouts in this scale with few problems. Predictably, 13.5mm and 14.2mm gauge standards have appeared, corresponding to EM and P4.

N GAUGE

N Gauge — currently the most popular size after 00 — has a track gauge of 9mm (the word for 'nine' in nearly all European languages begins with N) and a scale of 1/160 for Continental and American models. Once again, British N is different, having a scale of 1/148 or 21/16mm/ft. Prices are much the same as for 00 items and the range is nearly as wide.

2mm SCALE

2mm Scale, with a track gauge of 9.5mm, was first used some 50 years ago by a few experimental modellers. During the Second World War interest in the scale grew, due to the shortage of modelling materials, and the track gauge has since been refined to the exact scale figure of 9.42mm. The 2mm Scale Association provides a good range of essential parts, and some commercial N Gauge items and kits can be adapted — some kits are actually made to 2mm size.

Z GAUGE

Z Gauge is the smallest to appear on the scene. At present only Marklin and Kadee produce stock for this very small scale with a track gauge of 6.5mm and a scale of 1/220. Prices are higher than for the equivalent N gauge items.

As can be seen, the above scales use metric and imperial, ie. 4mm to the foot, so something 10 feet long in 4mm scale will measure 40mm. Now there is a pure scale that sits in between '0' gauge and H0/00 scale, and that is 'S' gauge which is 3/16in. to the foot.

S GAUGE

S Gauge uses a scale of $^3/_{16}$in/ft (1/64) and a gauge of $^7/_8$in. There is little commercial support, but the S Gauge Society provides a range of essential supplies. There is quite a large following of this scale in the United States which includes its own magazine.

Finally, just to confuse the issue further, are the Narrow Gauges. As a rule of thumb, the narrow gauge of one scale runs on track of the next scale down, for example '0' gauge (7mm/ft) narrow gauge runs on 00/H0 track. Other scale/gauge combinations use the scenic accessories and some rolling-stock parts from one scale with track and locomotive mechanisms from a smaller one. A few examples are:

1/24 scale on G1 track representing metre gauge (LGB)
16mm/ft scale on '0' Gauge track representing 2ft gauge
4mm scale on TT track representing 3ft or meter gauge
4mm scale on N track representing 2ft 3in gauge
2mm or N on Z track representing meter gauge

To try to simplify this vast array of facts and figures, we will take the three main scales '0', 00/H0 and N and say that something 8ft in '0' gauge will be 4ft in 00/H0 and only 2ft in N. This is the easiest way to look at it. Basically, the choice is yours and depends on the space, money and resources you have available, coupled to what you want your model railway to look like.

The layout we are building in this book measures 8ft long in 00/H0 scale, so it would be 4ft in N gauge and 16ft in '0' gauge . . . your choice.

4 WHAT'S AVAILABLE?

A well-stocked model shop is not a common sight these days. Model Images, shown here, can supply any of the products used in this book to personal callers, or by post.

Before planning your layout (the next chapter), take a look around your local model shop. When you see the range of sets, accessories, stock and scenic materials available, you should easily reach a decision. A particular model of a loco or train or even a kit for a building may appeal to you and point the way for your future model railway project.

By far the most popular gauge is 00/H0 and here the market leader is Hornby Model Railways. Produced in a factory in Margate, Kent, this manufacturer has been trading for many years under a variety of name changes. Some of these include

Tri-ang, Tri-ang/Hornby, Hornby/Tri-ang and, currently, Hornby. They have very kindly supplied a large number of the components for this project. Other manufacturers producing British outline model railways are Lima, Dapol, Replica and Bachmann.

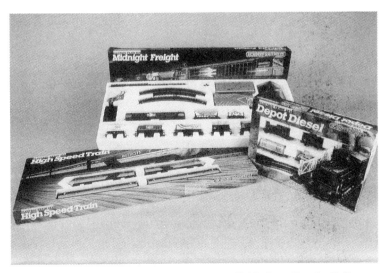

A selection of train sets ideal to start with, available from Hornby Railways. Their range includes steam, diesel and, soon, electric outline sets.

For the European modeller, both Marklin and Fleischmann are easily available in this country. American outline is available, but not to the same volume as the British outline.

That is the situation for the 00/H0 market. For N-gauge, the biggest manufacturer of British outline is Graham Farish, based at Poole in Dorset. The range covers both steam and modern image outline and now even includes overhead electric traction. Locos, coaches and rolling-stock are available for the various periods, and they really are superb models. Our layout is quite suited to N-gauge – simply halve the measurements. Minitrix also produce British outline which is imported into this country, and for the European modeller, once again Marklin and Fleischmann market excellent products including trackwork.

'0' gauge tends to be more a case of building your own stock from large ranges of kits from numerous manufacturers. Lima produce a limited range of ready-to-run stock in a number of different liveries.

Most of the aforementioned manufacturers have available

Lima Models also offer a range of train sets in varying sizes and even a complete layout. Most sets include some working feature; they have excellent 'play' value.

sets, ranging from the basic starter to the deluxe, and this can form the ideal basis for your project.

The set I used to start with is the 'Mighty Mallard'. Included in this is a circuit of track, the 'Mallard' 4-6-2 loco plus three coaches, a basic controller/transformer and service manual. In fact, all that is needed to get going. To this basic set I have added a number of points, pieces of track and accessories.

Both Hornby and Lima's sets are for the 00/H0 modeller. For N-gauge, Graham Farish offer a full range of sets including transformers, track and, of course, the trains. Again, full prototypes are covered: steam, diesel and electric.

Graham Farish market a complete range of stock based on all the prototype power sources, ie. steam, electric and diesel. Featured here are the 4-6-2 A3 'Flying Scotsman', class 91 overhead electric, and a class 47 in triple grey railfreight livery.

First take one train set; I started with Hornby Railways 'Mighty Mallard' set. This contains an A4 4-6-2 loco, three Gresley coaches in blood/custard livery and an oval of track, power clip and controller. Additional accessory includes a 'sound' cassette tape.

To complement the basic trains, there is an enormous range of accessories that can enhance your model railway and bring it to life. You may want to feature the countryside, so trees, hedges, fences and farm-type buildings are required, while a city-oriented model requires retaining walls, warehouses, large station buildings etc. All of these and more are available from many sources and various manufacturers.

5 DESIGN YOUR LAYOUT FIRST

The subtitle for this chapter would be 'don't fall into the age-old trap'. The biggest single failing of most layout designers is to take a board and then design a layout to fit it. Squeezing a bit here, stretching a bit there until it fits...No, most definitely NO! Design your layout first and, once its final design has been accepted, fit the woodwork around it. This way only minimal changes, if any, are required.

When designing your own layout there are several good publications available to give ideas. Pictured here are two from Hornby themselves, and the other from Patrick Stephens Ltd., by C J Freezer (be careful of the measurements in the latter as some of the curves are impractical).

First, list the requirements of the layout you want to build. For the layout I built, my list of requirements was as follows:

Mainline running — single circuit
Terminus station — with return loop
To accommodate a number of fixed trains — storage sidings
Each train to have two locos — plenty of loco shed space
Main controller and shunt controller — independent of each other.

From the main points above, I designed the resulting layout. Now, expanding the main points further, I'll show you the scope of this layout in both the type of stock it can carry and its potential operation.

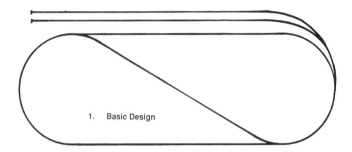

1. Basic Design

Simple circuit with reverse curve and terminus.

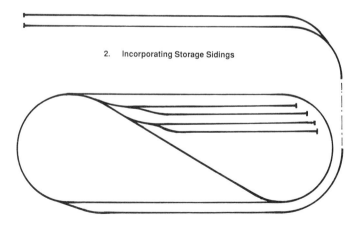

2. Incorporating Storage Sidings

Storage sidings need to be at a lower level with the terminus at a higher level.

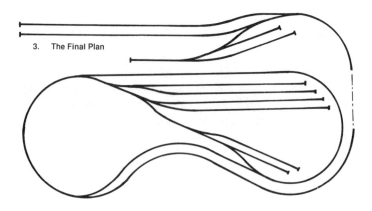

3. The Final Plan

This gives storage, mainline running, stock movements, terminus, loco sheds, banker and goods movements.

Starting with the terminus, I decided that a loco and three coaches was a reasonable length train to be accommodated in the platform. Also, there had to be enough room to hold the second engine that brought the train in. The main theme is running steam trains from different regions in the late British Railways period. This allows one train to have two locos, for example the 'Mallard' loco with train can also be paired with, say, the 'Flying Scotsman' loco. The requirement to run a number of different trains means that they need to be stored somewhere when not in use. This was resolved by a series of storage sidings under the main terminus on the lower level, giving a two level layout that will require the building of embankments, etc., up to the terminus.

One of the worst properties of train sets is the sharp radius curves, a necessary evil. Otherwise, layouts would need 4ft minimum curves which would make them very big, a factor that needs to be very seriously considered when entering 'fine scale' modelling. So, somehow these curves will have to be disguised just leaving the front centre section showing. Various scenic features can be used to hide the 'curves'; more on this later, but it is something that has to be considered at the planning stage.

Something not required, but usually present on a steam layout, is a turntable. Because we have a reverse curve, this accessory is not required as, when the loco is run through the reverse loop, it will in fact be facing the other way. It also takes up quite a lot of space and is fairly expensive; it is the sort of thing that can be added at a later date. Therefore, you must allow room to accommodate this, and it must be included on the basic plan; indicated in dotted lines, perhaps, as a later development.

It might be a particular feature that will form the centrepiece of your inspired layout. For me, it was the superb overall roof currently available from Hornby.

To hide the sharp curves at the ends, I decided to create a town at the terminus station end. Here, you can use the excellent Victorian shops and houses (again from Hornby). At the other end, some sort of mountain or hill will cover the two tracks; this will be a case of trial and error once the tracks have been laid.

As you can see, the planning stage of any layout project is very important and you have to take a great deal of care. As I mentioned earlier, try to include as much as you can on the plan, even down to the routes the wires will take for the electric points, and where the controller, electrical switches and point levers are situated.

Finally, always try to leave access to the main track circuits so that the layout can be extended at a later stage. While on this subject, the available space will govern the area the layout can occupy. Don't get carried away by trying to produce Euston or Paddington as your first layout. Start small to gain experience and then expand just like the real thing did in its formative years. You will see that a good layout, when finished off with proper drapes and ply edging, can be a prominent feature in a room — in fact, an attractive focal point.

6 THE PLAN

To accompany this book a full-size plan is available from Argus Plans at Argus House, Boundary Way, Hemel Hempstead, Herts, HP2 7ST, UK. This plan has all of the track components drawn out and numbered. Also marked on it is the wood framework of 2in × 1in timbers. Measurements for these timbers can be taken directly from this plan.
Wood required is:

2in × 1in × 8ft × 2
2in × 1in × 4ft × 4
2in × 1in × 3ft × 2
2in × 1in × 2ft × 3
2in × 1in × 2ft 6in × 2
1in × 1in × 8ft × 2
1in × 1in × 4ft × 4
1in × 1in × 1ft × 5
1in × 1in × 3ft × 1
Sundeala 4ft × 2ft (nominal) boards × 3
(one cut in half lengthways to give 2 × 1ft × 4ft)
15mm ply, 4ft × 2ft sheet

The above measurements are not exact, but will need to be adjusted slightly. These adjustments are, of course, available on the plan.
   We can now look at the track requirements for the project layout.

Included with the standard train set are:

8 × R605 Double Curve
4 × R600 Straight

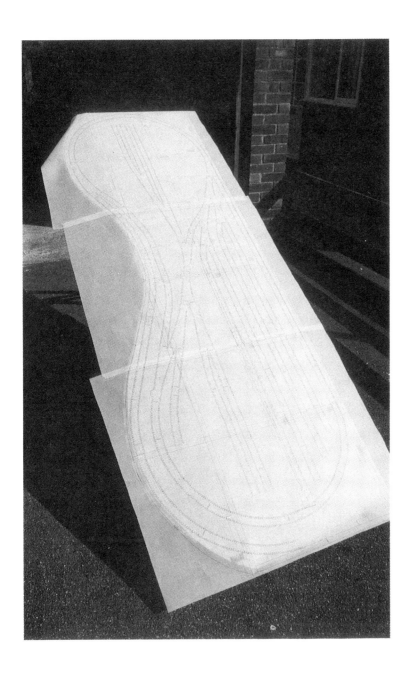

A full-sized plan containing track laid out and base frame cross-braces with dimensions. The plan is available from Argus Plans.

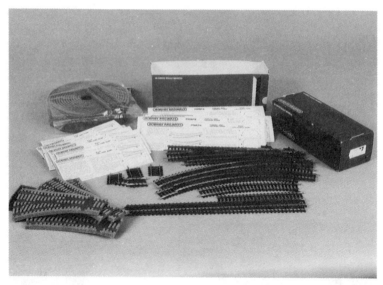

A full list of parts is included of the additional items needed, eg. points, track (both curved and straight) and underlay.

Track components required to complete this layout are:

10 × R600 Straight
16 × R601 Double Straight
9 × R603 Long Straight
5 × R604 Curve
2 × R605 Double Curve
2 × R606 Curve
4 × R607 Double Curve
4 × R608 Curve
16 × R610 Short Straight
4 × R612 Left Hand Point
4 × R613 Right Hand Point
6 × R622 Left Hand Express Point
3 × R623 Right Hand Express Point
6 × R628 Curve
1 × R640 Left Hand Curve Point
1 × R643 Half Curve

In addition, you will eventually need to electrify all 14 points but, for starting off, only five need to be connected. For this, Hornby have a R663 Point Remote Control Set. This includes a point motor that clips onto the side of the point, a passing contact switch and connecting wires. This unit can also be connected to a single semaphore signal. Power is taken from the 16 volt AC ancillary power supply available on the Tasma mains controller.

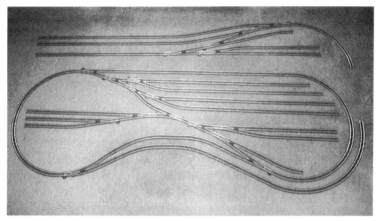

The initial track-plan had track in the centre areas as well. This was later modified to accommodate the Faller roadway (as the diagram below).

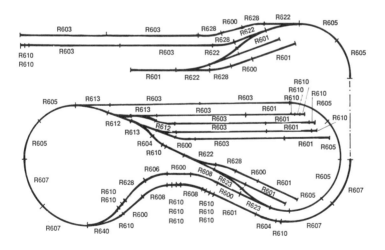

Hornby track component diagram.

Use the plan as a guide to identify the various track components that can be laid out onto the baseboard. The plan can also be used to place buildings, roadways and main scenic features.

7 MATERIALS & TOOLS

While power tools make the woodwork side of things a lot easier, ordinary hand tools are just as acceptable. Our basic list of tools is fairly small and I will run through some useful tips when using these tools. An elaborate workshop isn't necessary, just enough space to wield around 8ft lengths of wood.

The basic tools required for building the wooden sections of the layout. Power tools certainly make this part of the construction a lot easier.

The tools pictured include:

Black & Decker Jig Saw
Black & Decker Power Drill
Black & Decker Power Screwdriver
6in set square
12ft steel tape
sharp knife
Evostick wood glue (Resin W)
50 ¾in No 8 screws
100 1½in No 8 screws

There is also, of course, the old faithful — the Black & Decker Workmate. As for hand tools, an ordinary Tenon saw, screwdriver and hand drill will replace the power tools. For the Workmate, use a small table or even a chair, just as long as a G-clamp can be attached to hold the work steady. Its holding capabilities are the main use of the Workmate.

Use a square when marking up the lines. Always cut inside the marked line with the saw.

When cutting wood, always mark the line to be cut very clearly with a pencil and use a square to get the line perfect. The square is also used when making joints to ensure that the joint is at right angles.

If wood is to be interslotted, then once again mark the wood above where it is to be cut very clearly and even put a mark on the piece of wood to be discarded. After marking the work, use an offcut of wood to mark the thickness line and measure the half depth to be removed. Cut with the saw inside the marked lines so that the wood joint will fit firmly. You can clean up any ragged

When cutting joints, always cut inside the marks and then use a Stanley knife to remove the odd piece. Several light cuts from each side will give a neat cut.

edges with a craft knife. When removing a blind piece, use the knife and score the wood; several light cuts from both sides and the piece will pop out. Drill the holes to accept the screws in the piece of wood to be attached, and start off the screws. Then add a drop of wood glue to the other surface, hold the two pieces together and drive home the screws. Check with the square that all is at right angles and, should any adjustments be needed, remove the screws and correct. It is always best to use both glue and screws in the joints.

Pre-drill the holes required in the main spars, again using the squarely drawn line.

Start the screws off until they just appear on the underside. A drop of glue is then spread into the end to be attached and the joint can be completed.

8 CONSTRUCTION

We have now finally arrived at the construction stage of the baseboard. As I mentioned earlier, the measurements of the wood are only rough and should be finalized on the plan.

Components needed for the softwood main frame. The three 2 × 1in crosspieces fit in between the two 2 × 1in main rails, so they should be reduced to approximately 22in giving an overall width of 23½in.

Firstly, construct a frame using three of the 2ft 2 × 1in cross-pieces and two of the 8ft 2 × 1in main rails. The cross-pieces should fit inside the outer rails, with the overall width the same as the width of the sheet of Sundeala, which is something like

23½in. Same with the length — measure the combined length of two pieces of Sundeala butted up to each other. The front rail should have four half depth cut-outs in it to accept the four extended cross-braces that will support the front curved pieces of the baseboard. Notches in the front rail should face downwards when the frame is assembled.

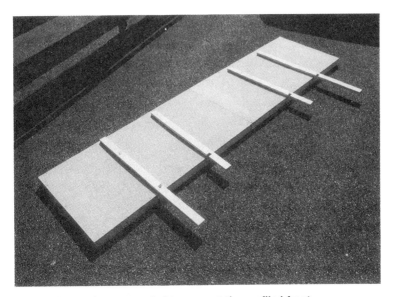

Extended cross-braces needed to support the profiled front.

Ensure that the framework fits to the edges of the boards all the way round. Also make sure that the framework is symmetrical, once again using the square for this job. Screw and glue all joints and the Sundeala to the frame.

One very important point when undertaking the woodwork, particularly when measuring and marking a line, is always to check the measurement carefully before cutting...it's hard to stick wood back on once it has been cut off!

Once the glue in the basic framework and surface has cured (about 30mins) then add the four longer cross-braces, making sure they fit flush to the board surface. If they don't, then gently trim the notches with a knife so that a good fit results. When you're happy, glue and screw them in place.

Extensions in place, the cut-outs face down on the main pieces.

A completed leg with 1 × 1in. strengtheners on 2 × 1in. frame.

Now take a look at the legs. Once again, these are 2 × 1in frames with cross-pieces, but this time 1 × 1in lengths have been screwed and glued to the legs; this greatly stiffens the legs, giving more stability.

Legs mounted to the base with hinges.

Now for the all-important diagonal folding stays that will allow the legs to be folded up and down. Once the legs have been attached, noticing that they will fold one inside the other (see sketch), you can work out the stay measurements. When the legs are in the upright position, measure between leg cross-brace and a suitable layout cross-brace (eg. the resulting measurement is 20in). Then fold the leg down to the board and note the relative positions of these cross-braces. If they coincide (lucky!), then just halve the stay length and add three back flap hinges. If, as is usual, the cross-braces are out, measure this distance difference. Say it is 4in, then subtract this from the main figure of 20in resulting in 16in. This is then halved to give two 8in. Add the difference, 4in to one side giving two pieces of wood, one 12in the other 8in. Add three back flap hinges and you have a folding stay.

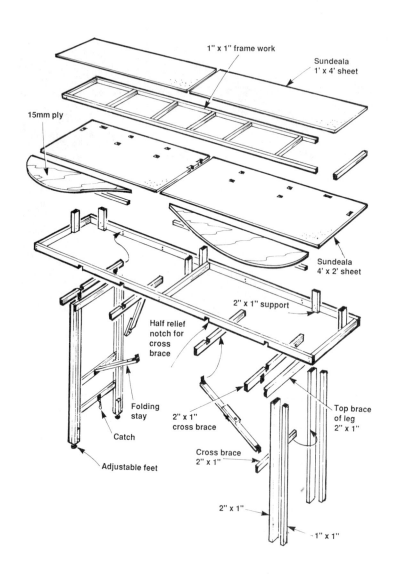

1" x 1" frame work

Sundeala
1' x 4' sheet

15mm ply

Sundeala
4' x 2' sheet

2" x 1" support

Half relief
notch for
cross
brace

Folding
stay

2" x 1"
cross brace

Catch

Cross brace
2" x 1"

Adjustable feet

Top brace
of leg
2" x 1"

2" x 1"

1" x 1"

Exploded diagram of baseboard sections.

Arrangement for locking cross-brace, coach bolt and wingnut secure assembly.

To lock the stay in the upright position, fit a smaller piece of wood secured to one side of the folding stay with screws and a coach bolt through the other side. This allows the stay to lock-out giving a firm stable base. We now have a free standing base-board.

Profiled extensions are from 15mm ply (the hole at the bottom is an error. . . oops!).

The front curves are made from 15mm ply, this being a rigid material that won't sag and can be screwed straight onto the protruding cross-braces. It is shaped to the profile of the track diagram which is on our plan.

Framework for upper level terminus is made from 1 × 1 in. softwood.

Complete baseboards finished. Upper, lower and profile extensions.

We can now look at the upper level which uses a 1in × 1in framework supported on pieces of wood screwed to the main base's cross-braces. These come up through holes cut in the Sundeala surface; again, all of this information is on the published plan. The Sundeala surface for this can then be cut and screwed on, but not glued as it will have to be removed for the track underneath to be laid. Also, note where you are going to position the transformer/controller, in our case a twin unit from

Pre-drill holes in the cross-braces to receive wiring looms later.

Tasma. Put in all relevant holes to take the wires for the controllers and point levers at this point; both through the Sundeala baseboard and the wooden cross-braces on both upper and lower levels.

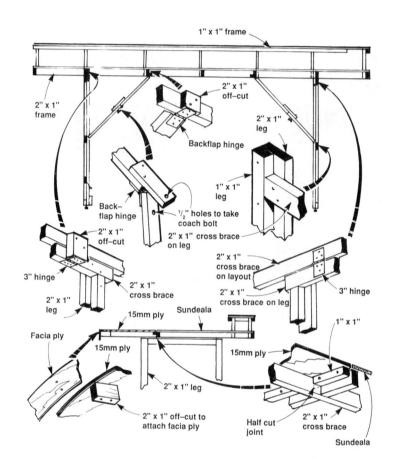

Exploded diagram of various joints used on the baseboard.

Finally, add small pieces of 2 × 1in wood around the curved edges of the thick plywood at the front; this will hold the cosmetic ply secured to them later for the curved front.

One of the adjustable foot units to keep the baseboard level.

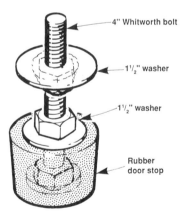

4" Whitworth bolt

$1\frac{1}{2}$" washer

$1\frac{1}{2}$" washer

Rubber
door stop

Adjustable foot.

A refinement you might like to add to your layout is a set of adjustable feet. These are made from large 4in bolts with one nut welded to a large washer while the bolt passes through a door stop held in position by another nut and washer. Another refinement is a further cross-brace which can be added to the

An additional cross-brace is added to one leg in order to fix catch.

outer leg when the legs are in the folded-up position. Line it up with a cross-brace on the main frame and secure it with screws to the leg; you can then add an eye and catch clip. This will stop the legs dropping down during transit of the baseboard. A carabena clip will secure the catch clip.

9 PERMANENT WAY

Having now achieved a folding platform that should stop your creation from hitting the floor(!), the trackwork can be laid, centred on the shaped baseboard and located with pins. Here

The track is secured to the baseboard with pins. A track pinning tool is ideal for this job.

the use of a track pinning tool will greatly speed up the process — not to mention the lack of disturbance caused when a hammer and centre punch are used, and the track just jumps everywhere.

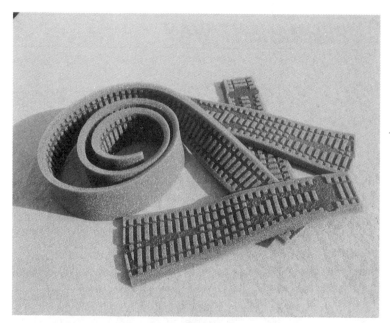

Foam underlay is available from Hornby and Peco. Some simple cutting is required on the Peco items to fit Hornby points.

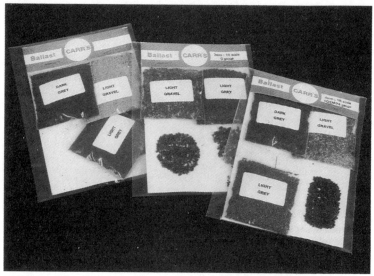

Carr's Products offer an extensive range of ballasts in different scales and colours.

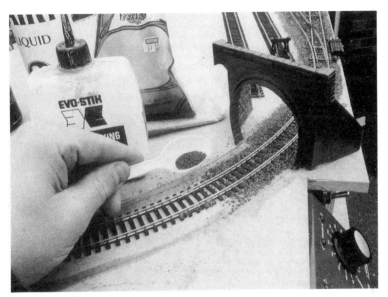

Applying ballast to the upper level with a spoon, a small area at a time. Lightly tap the ballast onto the track.

Once the ballast is in position it can be retained with wood glue (Resin W) which has been diluted 50/50 with water and had several drops of washing-up liquid added.

On this layout I have used two methods of ballasting for trackwork. On the lower base level, where there are continuous train movements for prolonged periods, I have used foam underlay which cuts down the noise. The underlay used is available from Hornby and Peco, although some tedious carving will be required to the Peco point underlays to fit the Hornby points. Short underlays are required for R612 or R613 points and medium underlays for R622 and R623 points.

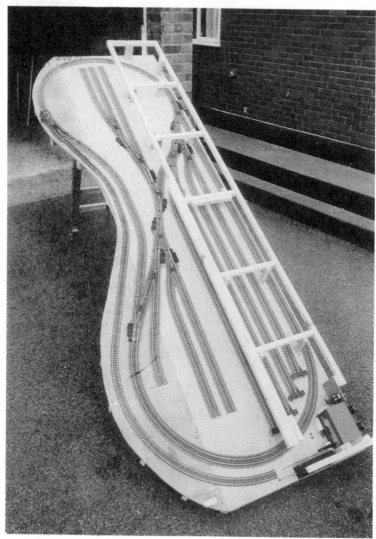

The lower level trackwork is laid on foam underlay as it provides quieter running. (The sidings layout shown is an alternative to that which I used.)

On the upper level scale, ballasting has been used. This does take quite a time to do, but the final effect is worth it. Carefully spread the ballast (in this case from Woodland Scenics), then, to secure it, use a 50/50 diluted mixture of Evostick wood glue (Resin W) with water. If you add a few drops of washing-up liquid to the mixture, it will remove the surface tension of the water and allow the glue to spread through the ballast easily. When gluing, be careful around the point switch blades as you don't want glue in them (this is the single, most often made mistake).

Upper level trackwork shows the site of the two road running sheds for locos.

Firstly, lay the trackwork as indicated on the plan on the lower level. Once laid out, the underlay can be fitted in and pinned all the way round. Once this has been achieved, the manual points

Entrance pointwork to the hidden storage sidings on the lower level showing point remote control sets fitted. Check uprights for stock clearance.

Sprung hydraulic buffers are glued onto the ends of the hidden storage roads.

are electrified using R663 Point Remote Control Sets. The electric point motors simply clip to the side of the points and a relevant hole is drilled to take the wires to the motor. The upper level board can then be added, this time screwed and glued into position, and once dry the trackwork can be added.

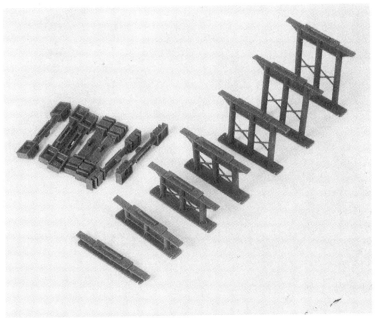

A set of Hornby piers was used to get a reasonably smooth incline from the lower to upper level.

This leaves the link track between the two levels. This will be a mixture of embankment and steel piers. So, to start with, the incline is carefully packed up using R658 Inclined Piers to get a smooth gradual incline. Also used are R659 High Level Piers. Embankments will be filled in later.

The only alteration to the rail joints (fishplate) is the reverse loop section indicated on the plan. At both ends of the central section, the metal fishplates have to be removed and insulated plastic ones substituted. This will electrically isolate that section which will be wired up later.

To enhance the track's appearance, the sides of the rails and the chairs that hold the rail in place should be painted a rust or track colour. This hides that awful bright steel colour.

Incline with piers is seen on the left. This also shows the simplified lower level trackwork to that seen on page 52.

The centre section known as the reverse loop needs insulated fishplates at its extremes. These are available from Peco and easily replace the metal ones.

To add realism to the track, paint the rail both sides with a rust colour. This is a lengthy process, but well worth the effort.

After painting the track and gluing the ballast, a good clean-up is required. For this I used the Fleischmann track rubber; others are available, but avoid wet and dry paper.

The choice of venue of the layout will also govern the choice of type of track. I used Hornby track which has steel rail, as this is more suited to indoor layouts. It would not be too good, however, in a garage, where it is rather damp and rust could be a problem. For this venue, nickel silver track, available from Peco, would be much better suited.

10 WIRING UP

I have purposely kept the electrics to a minimum on this layout, as more and more people I encounter relate tales of difficult experiences in this area.

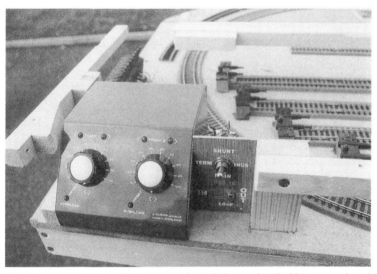

The Tasma controller with home-made switch panel to hold 'reverse loop' switch and controller to different sections selection.

Having said that, they are simple, very flexible and will enable multi-train movements and, of course, add interest. The terminus, circuit and return loop are all fully isolated from each other by the insertion of Peco insulated fishplates, as shown on the circuit plan. Using double pole, double throw switches on each circuit, the two controllers can be switched to either of the track sections.

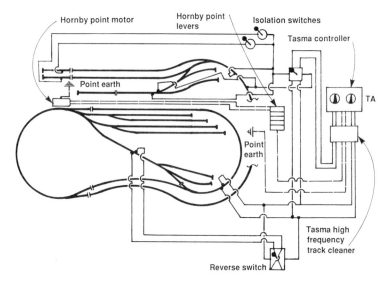

Basic layout wiring diagram.

Hornby point motor and switch kit used to motorize points. A full wiring diagram is included.

The reverse loop is wired into the base circuit wiring through another DPDT switch, but this time acting as a changeover switch with the following movement taking place. The entrance points are switched and the changeover switch set in the 'down' position. The train enters the centre track and stops at the end tunnel mouth. The train can then either be reversed back into the storage sidings or the changeover switch pushed over along with the incline point, the transformer reversed and the train can then move off up to the station. The enter point is then returned to normal ready for the next train to enter the circuit. Once in the circuit, the two controllers can be returned to separate sections for dual train control.

The storage sidings, this time showing the point motors in place and wired up. Once the top surface is fitted, access to these points will be restricted.

Turning now to the points, with the point motor already in place and the hole already drilled to receive the wires. The point switches (black) are clipped together and are similar to a bank of levers in a signal box. With points nearest to the switches the wires included in the kit will be long enough to reach to connect both. Simply plug the red and green wires into both the motor and switch.

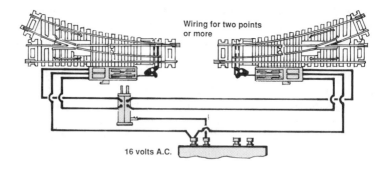

Wiring for two points or more

16 volts A.C.

Wiring diagram for Hornby point motors.

Now look at the black lead which is connected to all the point motors. I have run several lengths of self-adhesive copper tape along four of the cross-braces on the main baseboard. The various black wires can then be soldered to them and a single wire connecting all four can also run to the 16 volt AC supply on the transformer. The other terminal of the 16 volt AC supply on the transformer connects to the back of the point switches. Test the points for smooth operation and decide on a normal position for the points. If a point direction has to be changed, then simply swap over the red and green wires to the point motor.

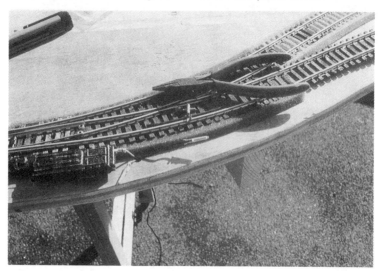

For motors further away than the wires included in the kit, new ones need to be made up. The solder type bullets are available separately.

For those point motors further away from the levers than the length of the wires provided, you will have to make up new wires. Soldered bullets are available separately from your local model shop, as are the different coloured wires. Try to retain the original colours of green, red and black. Thread the wires through the holes in the cross-braces of the baseboard and cut to length. Strip about ½in off the outer casing, twist the wires and push into the bullet. With a pair of pliers crimp the ends and then, with a soldering iron, fill the bullet with solder.

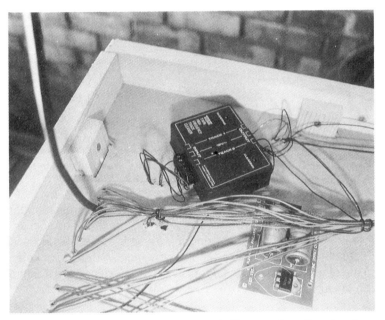

Tasma also do a Twin High Frequency Track Cleaner, where the wires from the controller are simply connected straight through the unit.

Two additional electronic boxes have been added to this layout to aid more efficient operation. Firstly, a Tasma twin high frequency track cleaner has been wired into the controller system. This is much easier to wire up than other similar units as it allows the 16 volt supply that is used to power it to be further used to work the points previously mentioned. Secondly, connected into the point circuit is a capacitor discharge unit. This makes the electric point motors (solenoids) move with more of a thump.

Wiring has been kept simple. Make the soldered connections to the metal fishplates. Use flux, along with 4-core solder, to get a good joint.

The only other electrical connections to be made are a number of isolating sections on the layout, mainly in the terminus section. These allow the locos that bring the trains in to be isolated and uncoupled from their trains. Another engine can then be coupled to the other end of the train, then, when ready, depart back round the layout.

11 ELECTRICS EXPLAINED

Nearly all present-day 00, H0 or N gauge model railways are powered by 12 volt direct current (DC) on the 2-rail system, the exception being Marklin H0 which uses 14 volt AC and stud contact.

In the 2-rail system, the rails are insulated from each other by the plastic sleeper base. Current flows along one running rail, through the wheels on that side of the locomotive to the motor, and then back through the wheels on the other side and other running rail. The advantages of this system are realism — there are no conductor rails which are not there in the prototype — and the fact that the whole of the locomotive's weight is available for adhesion and contact, no power being wasted in dragging along a contact shoe or skate. This becomes more important as the models get smaller.

Some makers offer the option of overhead current collection on models of electric locos which are powered this way. However, for the beginner it is probably best to start with 2-rail anyway; the overhead wiring can be added later and conversion of the wiring is very simple.

POWER SUPPLY

The power supply for model railways almost always comes from the mains via a transformer. The use of alternating current mains makes it possible to step the 240 volts of the mains down to a safe 12-18 volts. The AC output of the transformer cannot drive a motor directly (except for the Marklin ones referred to above) and so must be turned into direct current or rectified. In addition, control of direction and speed is necessary; these three functions are normally combined in the controller which is supplied with most boxed train sets.

Permanent-magnet motors are reversed simply by reversing the flow of current; in most controllers, this is done by means of a double-pole two-way switch. The simplest form of speed control is a variable resistance — a length of resistance wire wound on a former with a metal or carbon brush arranged to slide along it — connected in series with the motor; this controls the current through the circuit and so varies the speed of the train.

The complete circuit for a simple layout (say a plain oval of track) is shown in Fig. 1. The components are drawn as symbols

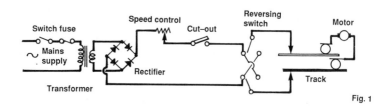

Fig. 1

Fig. 1 Diagram showing how the mains voltage forming the normal household circuit is reduced to an acceptable level suitable for model railways.

which suggest their function rather than what they actually look like (the rectifier, for example, is probably a plastic blob with four wires sticking out, but the symbol shows the individual cells or diodes as little arrowheads, suggesting one-way flow). Wires are drawn as plain lines. This is a sort of shorthand used by electricians to make circuits easier to understand, and it's as well to get used to it. Looking at this diagram, you should be able to see how the AC mains is stepped down, rectified into DC and fed to the motor via the speed control and reversing switch.

A cut-out is also shown; this is a magnetic or heat-sensitive device designed to break the circuit if the current rises much above that drawn by a normal locomotive — as may happen, for example, if the rails are 'short-circuited' together by derailed rolling-stock or a dropped screwdriver. Many controllers include something of the sort.

POINTS AND SIDINGS

Most layouts include pointwork and sidings, and here we meet the first real problem with the 2-rail system. At the 'frog' or 'crossing', a rail from one side of the track crosses over one from the other side. They must not touch, or there would be a 'short circuit' — the current from the controller would pass straight from one rail to the other and there would be no voltage available for the trains. In most commercial points, this is dealt with by making the crossing of plastic and fitting wire links under the base to feed the current across the gap (Fig. 2). A train travelling fairly

Fig. 2 Basic wiring for a self-isolating point (frog current is switched via the point blades).

fast on either track can pick up current from the wheels on either side of the break, or 'coast' for a short distance if contact should be lost for a moment.

Unfortunately, it isn't that simple. One of the delights of running a model railway is to carry out train movements at 'scale' speeds, making the models move slowly and smoothly to suggest the massive weight of the real thing. At these speeds, however, the model has virtually no coasting ability, and the slightest break in the supply — caused by a spot of dirt or a bit of 'dead' rail — will cause it to stop. In most commercial locos, the wheels are not sprung, and so, however many wheels a loco has, only three are likely to be actually touching the track at any moment. If one of these is on the plastic crossing, the loco will stall.

You can do several things to overcome this. You can add a flywheel to the motor to enable it to 'coast' further at low speed; you can add pick-ups to those wheels of the loco (especially bogie and pony-truck wheels if it has any) which are not already provided with them. But the easiest move — since it doesn't involve taking locos to pieces — is to use 'live-frog' pointwork.

Live-frog points have the crossing made of metal, but separated from the rest of the rails by insulating gaps. Current reaches the crossing via a switch operated by the lever that sets the points, so that it is connected to the rail of which it forms a part whichever way the points are set. In commercial points, the switching is done by the point blades making contact with the stock rails; a more certain method is to use an electrical switch as a point lever and use it to switch the crossing. Fig. 3 shows

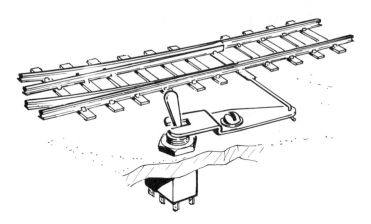

Fig. 3 Toggle switch used as a mechanical point lever.

a way of doing this; the reversing lever is included to make the 'dolly' of the switch point the same way as the turnout setting. Live-frog turnouts are available in both 00/H0 and N gauges, though the range is not as extensive as for the dead-frog type.

POINT OPERATION

On a small layout, you can set the points by hand, since they will all be within easy reach of the operator. As the layout gets larger — or the amount of delicate scenery such as signals, telegraph poles or overhead wiring makes it more difficult to reach the track — some sort of remote control becomes necessary.

Point motors usually consist of two electromagnets, between which an iron core slides back and forth. There is usually a locking device — a pin in a lazy-Z slot or an over-centre spring — to prevent the points from being forced over against the setting of the motor. Because the magnets are small, they are not very efficient and require a lot of current to produce enough force to throw the points; if this current continued to flow for more than a second or two, the coils would get very hot and burn out. Thus, point motors are operated by 'passing contact' switches or pairs of push-buttons; the power supply is usually AC taken directly from a 16 volt output on the transformer.

A cheaper substitute for many push-buttons or switches required for a large layout is the 'electric pencil'. A diagram of the layout is painted or taped on a sheet of plywood, hardboard or Formica and at each turnout two brass screws are fixed, wires leading from them behind the panel to the point motor. The 'pencil' itself consists of an insulating holder, such as an old ballpoint pen, the refill being replaced by a piece of brass rod or thick wire glued in and provided with a flexible wire to the transformer. Touching the tip of the 'pencil' to the screwheads provides a pulse of current to either side of the point motor as required. A refinement is a 'holster' in which the pencil can be parked when not in use, to prevent it from making contact with any metal parts which might cause a short circuit.

WIRING UP

So far we have assumed that the current feed reaches the locomotive only via the rails. This is generally satisfactory in small layouts, where the distance from any point on the track to the feed point is less than 10ft (3m) for 00/H0 and 6ft (2m) for N. In larger layouts, however, the resistance of the rails becomes significant, not to mention the number of fishplate joints if sectional track is used. Some thought should be given to providing additional feeds at intervals, using insulated copper wires of, say, 16/0.2mm or 24/0.2mm gauge run under the baseboard and connected to the rails by 'droppers' every so often. Ideally, each piece of rail should have its own 'dropper' so that current feed does not rely on the fishplates at all.

A small layout can be built up without soldering, track connections being taken care of by the rail joiners and connection to the rails being via a 'terminal rail' which is usually included in boxed sets. Sooner or later, as the layout grows, soldering will become necessary; there is a limit beyond which fishplates and 'twiddle' joints cannot be relied on. There is nothing to be concerned about, for we are dealing with two of the most easily soldered metals.

The commonest reason for poor soldered joints is insufficient heat. The iron must be hot enough and have sufficient mass to heat the metals to be joined quickly to the melting point of solder; many small irons designed for miniature electronic wiring do not satisfy this requirement. A 25 watt iron of reputable make, with a small 'chisel' bit, will cover most of the modeller's needs in 00 or N gauge.

Put a small blob of 60/40 resin-cored solder on the iron and use it to trap the wire against the foot of the rail, and within a second or two it should be seen to 'flow' onto the rail. Touch the end of the solder wire to the spreading patch of solder, withdraw the iron and hold the wire in place until the solder goes 'misty' — and then for another ten seconds. (The second commonest cause of bad joints is allowing the parts to move before the solder has properly hardened.)

The result should be a neat joint, with both rail and wire well 'wetted' with bright solder, but with not too big a blob. Practise on a spare piece of track until you can make this sort of joint every time without overheating the plastic base; it isn't difficult because heat spreads quite slowly through the rail.

A similar technique is used for wire-to-wire joints or those between wires and the tags of components such as switches. In the latter case, it is usual to twist the wire lightly round the tag to hold it in place while soldering. Don't twist it too tight — you may need to take it off again one day! Feed wires are best brought up through small holes drilled in the baseboard, close to the rail on the side away from the normal viewing position, and soldered to the rail foot. When the track is painted, such joints are almost invisible.

As the layout grows, the wiring will become more complex as it is installed. Use a notebook to list the start and finish of each wire and its colour. An orderly approach like this will make it much easier to repair the system if anything goes wrong.

12 SCENICS

Once the trackwork has been laid, wired and is working, then the next stage is the scenics. It is this medium that will transform your train set into a model railway — your own piece of history captured in miniature.

The finished model, looking down the high street towards the station. These are the finished Hornby Victorian buildings.

The first thing to consider is how you are going to hide the curves at the ends of the layout; in actual fact they are more like corners so they need to be disguised. With the alterations to the basic track diagram now to incorporate a working Faller model

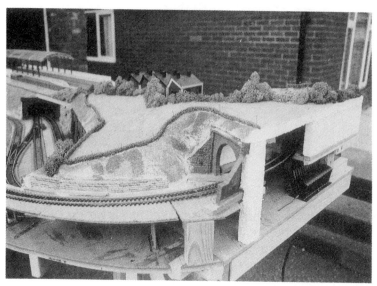

Opposite end to the town scene is the hill which covers the tight curves. Behind the hill and hidden from the front view is the turning circle for the Faller roadway.

roadway system, you can use hills and scenery to enhance the whole thing.

Using the roadway as an inspiration for hills, you first have to decide the route the road will take. One single circuit will allow bi-directional working down the main road in the centre of the layout; with single direction working around the return loop ends.

I decided that the roadway would thread its way around the town outside the station. I also needed the roadway to disappear at the other end in order to make the illusion more believable. When viewed from the front, a large hill rising from the centre towards the right hand end will hide the roadway, and there is enough room to accommodate a reverse loop...more on that later.

So, to recap, we have a town scene at one end, using the excellent Hornby Victorian shops and houses, and a large hill at the other end, giving a good view of the terminus on top and the incline and running line below.

The first job is the siting of the tunnel mouths that mark the entry and exit to the scenic breaks etc. When the track is on the flat, the plastic mouldings can easily be stuck to the base. This will be just below the town, inside the incline and on top above

Once the curves are laid, mark the clearance for the stock. Hold a pen at the centre of a coach and mark the baseboard.

Plastic tunnel mouths are available for single and double track. They have embossed stonework which can be realistically painted.

The tunnel mouths mark the extremes of the scenic breaks and are glued to the baseboard or sub-bases as required.

the controls. Where the inclined track enters the hill, an intermediate small base will have to be fixed up, big enough to take the tunnel mouth. The only other entrance is on the reverse curve line and siding, and here a double track tunnel mouth is required. The others mentioned were singles. The small base needed for the inclined track was a piece of ply held up by two offcuts of 2in × 1in screwed and glued to the baseboard.

The embossed retaining wall is from Langley, while the rock face is castings taken from a cork bark mould.

Having now established the limits, take a look at other major scenic features, such as rock faces and retaining walls. Rock faces can be easily simulated using cork bark available from the larger florists or garden centres. The ones I used are, in fact, resin castings that were taken from a rubber mould which I made using a Strand Glass resin casting kit. My rock faces are straight, curved inwards and outwards. This is easily achieved with a rubber mould and allows more flexibility in designing terrain; just support the mould differently when casting and *voilà!* (This is only really necessary if you plan to build a number of layouts.)

The retaining walls are a plastic vacuum forming produced by Langley Miniature Models. Simply trim the wall and lightly tape it in place, then build the remaining terrain around it.

The large space behind the loco shed is the turning circle for the vehicles on the Faller roadway.

The remainder is formed from pieces of polystyrene glued together in layers forming the embankments and hills between the tunnel mouths. I use glue specially designed for use with polystyrene ceiling tiles, available from Texas Homecare Stores.

The base for the town and hill were made out of shaped Sundeala suitably supported above the lower tracks. The poly-styrene is glued to this.

Polystyrene is loosely cut and shaped then glued together with special polystyrene tile adhesive.

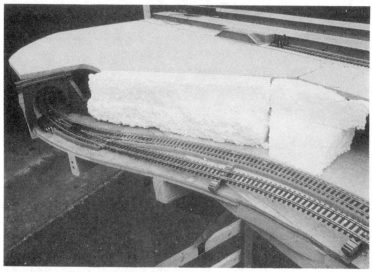

Once the blocks are in position and glued, a piece of Sundeala is cut and shaped to fit the required area.

Once the glue has dried (I would suggest a couple of days to make sure), judicious carving of the polystyrene layers can take place. I use a large carving knife and only take off thin layers at a time; too big a cut and you'll rip the styrene. It doesn't have to be a precise finished piece of work as you can fill in the gaps and cracks with plaster once the carving is complete. Be careful with the knife, as 'red martian landscapes' aren't too authentic on British style layouts (in other words don't cut yourself — take care with the blade). As already mentioned, use plaster to give a smooth surface to the bulk of the scenery. There should be realistic cracks and crevices for wildlife, such as fox holes or rabbit warrens, etc.

The polystyrene layers don't need to be profiled as, when the glue is dry, they are shaped with a suitable knife.

Once profiled the terrain is given a coat of plaster both to fill in the cracks and to give the polystyrene a protective covering.

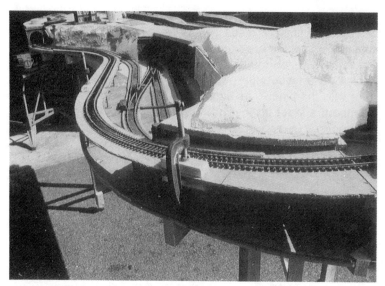

The incline's base is pieces of plywood that have been spliced together and then glued to the Hornby piers.

One further area which needs attention is the inclined track connecting the base circuit to the upper level terminus. I initially used the inclined Hornby pieces to give a realistic slope. Now you will need to mark, cut out and fit in a shaped plywood trackbed. Mine was made up of several bits joined together with glue and a stretcher piece clamped in position until the glue (Resin W) is set. Just before gluing in place, shape some polystyrene to fit between the piers then, using polystyrene tile glue (from Texas) and UHU on the piers, stick on the ply base. The track can then be relaid, pinned, ballasted and painted (that's rust colour on the sides of the rails).

It's now time to sprinkle a little colour into the growing work of art, and here the Crown emulsion paint tester pots are absolutely ideal. Use emulsion which is water-based, since this won't attack the polystyrene scenic base. Other spirit-based paints will attack and destroy your works of art, not to mention the scenery. Even though the colours are quite weak, they serve the purpose of covering up the great white areas. I used light green for the proposed grass areas, and painted other areas with a fawn/brown colour. The only other area of paint that requires attention is the rails. When laid, they are a bright steel colour whereas, in proto-type practice, rails are rusty. I used Humbrol brick red, liberally

After the plaster has dried thoroughly the various areas can be painted with emulsion test pots.

painted onto the rail sides using thinners to allow it to spread over the chairs and partially onto the ballast directly underneath. This one operation alone, while tedious, will completely transform the look of the track.

You cannot teach someone colour appreciation – it's either there or not – but you can show how it can be achieved. It is difficult to illustrate in black and white the application of colour, and particularly the build-up of layers of scatter colours, but this is fully covered in a Chess Valley video I undertook several years ago entitled 'How to Build a Model Railway', priced at £24.95, inclusive of VAT and postage. VHS copies can be obtained direct from Chess Valley at Film House, Little Chalfont, Bucks. (02402 2222). A brief general explanation of the techniques used in achieving the end result follows, while the pictures will help to tell part of the story.

Onto the painted landscape, brush some diluted PVA adhesive, that has had several drops of washing-up liquid added to it (this breaks the surface tension and allows the glue to spread quickly), a small area at a time, then, using a fairly coarse dyed sawdust, sprinkle it over the glued area. Cover the whole of the intended green areas with this scatter and allow it to dry thoroughly. The reason for using the coarse scatter is that, under the next layer of flocks to be applied, the base covering will hold a lot more glue being soaked up by the coarse sawdust particles.

It is difficult to show scenics in black and white, but the various techniques are covered in a video I made with Chess Valley.

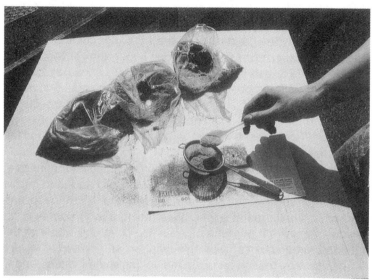

For the grass areas three different colours can be mixed in a tea strainer to give a varied hue.

The areas to be 'grassed' need to be glued first with the old faithful 50/50 wood glue/water mix. The grass can then be tapped into the various areas.

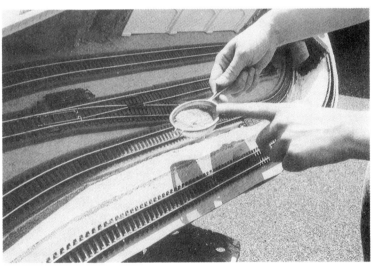

When coating embankments, tip the layout on to its side then glue and add the grass as before. Successive layers are best applied in the normal position.

To achieve an overall grass effect, I mixed three shades of green, then carefully applied this with the aid of a small tea strainer (available from any store). Don't have one overall green throughout the layout; vary it. Put darker green on steep embankments and lighter greens on the fields. Try starting with the medium green in the centre, the lighter green sprinkled either side, then the final, very light green carefully and lightly dusted over the whole lot just to give a highlight effect. I applied a link colour, in this case a speckled stone/brown flock, with a teaspoon between the greens and along the edge of the track ballast.

When all the layers have been added and the glue is dry, remove the excess grass with a vacuum cleaner.

For steep embankments, tilt the whole of the layout forward or backward so that the area you intend to sprinkle is near horizontal. Rest it on, say, a Black & Decker Workmate (see Chapter 7) or volunteer a couple of willing helpers to hold the layout while flock is glued and sprinkled on. Do this for the first covering only; subsequent layers should be glued and sprinkled in the normal position, as this will allow realistic layers to build up. Good scenics take time to achieve – it won't happen overnight so be patient.

A further useful item which you can add right at the end is some of the Noch electrostatic grass. Using their own puff bottles, the grass (small lengths of coloured nylon) is blown onto a previously glued area – the best glue for this job is photographic spray mount adhesive. Just pick out several small areas; this will be more effective than large ones.

BUSHES AND SHRUBS

Additional material suitable for hedges, walls, trees, etc., includes lichen, rubberized horse hair, coated wire wool and Resin W.

Rubberized horse hair makes ideal hedgerows. Cut a three inch strip from the supplied block (Scalelink or Jack Kine can supply this item) and tease it out until it's woolly looking. Then, using neat Resin W (white glue wood adhesive), fix to the landscape. Next, liberally coat the bush base and then, using Woodland Scenic foliage, which again has been stretched out, lightly press these pieces onto the base. Vary the colours slightly, and, as a final touch, add a mauve, dark red or even a pink coloured scatter material in small lumps to represent hedgerow flowers.

For ivy around tunnel mouths, use the spray mount direct onto the brickwork, then apply the teased-out Woodlands Scenic foliage again.

Hedgerows can be simulated using lichen. Carefully selected pieces are glued to the base and supported with cocktail sticks glued in.

The hillside is starting to look alive with the walling following the contours of the landscape.

Stone walling, available in three foot lengths, is also applied using neat Resin W and pinned upright until the glue is dry.

There are several ranges of trees on the market and here cost will govern your choice. Let me try to persuade you to go for the better quality, more expensive tree. Only one or two large realistic trees are needed, strategically placed to act as the centre of attention on the layout. Then simply use basic shrubs and hedges of lichen suitably secured with glued cocktail sticks on the rest of the layout.

If you make a tree the centre of interest, ensure it's a good one. This one is available from Model Masters.

Trees can be added at any stage as and when funds allow, so wait and use the better, more realistic items – it's worth it. I've only used three large trees and they are really effective, when suitably placed. Model Masters of Weston-Super-Mare supplied these examples; their range is extensive both in size and different types of trees.

To simulate scrubland, simply chop up some of the offcuts from the lichen etc.

Scenics is a matter of choice and experimenting. Don't use just one colour, mix several, be daring and if you don't like the result, try again; you can cover over with different coloured flocks, and get more depth.

Finally, once all the scenics have been completed, apply a judicious bit of weathering to the whole layout, particularly around the track area where dust and spray from the passing trains is deposited on the embankments, trackside buildings, bridges etc. Don't forget the black soot/smoke stains on the centres of the tunnel mouths; once again, observe the real thing and then experiment with reproducing it in model form.

Lightly glue the field that will have the treatment and sprinkle the mixture over it, allowing clumps to form.

13 ARCHITECTURE

In this section I have included station structures, service buildings such as engine sheds and ancillaries, houses and other general detailing equipment.

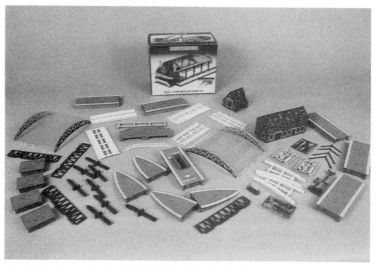

All the components included in the Hornby Railways R331 London Road Station. Other platform and canopy sections are required for our layout.

Once the track has been laid, making sure there is ample clearance for the platforms, you can glue them in position using neat Resin W wood glue. Just run a pencil line along both sides of the platforms, then glue down these lines and fit them in place. Secure with several screws through the canopy holes and allow to dry overnight, then the screws can be taken out.

For me, the main feature of this layout is the overall roof. I built up five units and joined them together with Plastic Weld glue, both along the joining seams and the supports to the platform (it's good glue). There then remain some unsightly holes in the platform, which should be filled and painted grey once the filler is dry. This imposing structure will become the centrepiece of the layout. It will eventually require some careful weathering.

To add strength to the overall roof structure, glue the units to each other using Plastic Weld (be careful of the fumes).

Now look at the roadways and walling. Faller, the excellent German buildings kit manufacturer, offers an extensive range of embossed pre-coloured sheets. I've chosen the cobbled sheets and the sandstone walling. As they are pre-painted and weathered, you can simply mark them up, cut and stick down using Copydex glue.

As a guide to the layout of the town, place the Faller cobblestone street sheets out, along with a pair of Hornby Victorian semi-detached houses.

Firstly, lay out the roadways giving attention to space and accommodating shops and houses that will be built and positioned later on. Do not stick them down at this stage.

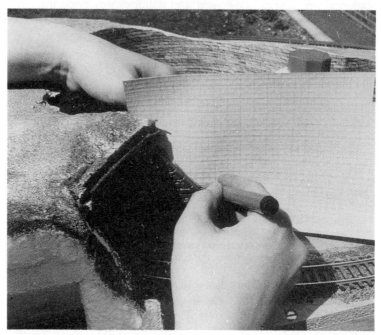

Stonework sheets are also available from Faller which can be marked up to cover walls.

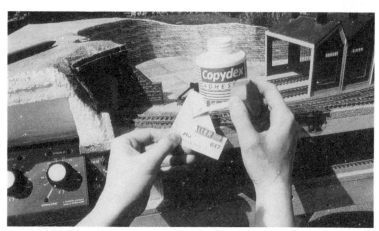

A retaining wall section has been cut out and is now having Copydex glue pasted onto it.

The walling is now in place on the wing wall of the tunnel mouth. Cobblestone sheets are on the road.

Once the walling has been applied there are gaps at the top that need filling. I used polystyrene tile glue from Texas Homecare.

For the tunnel mouth side walls, and other walls around the roadway, you need to mark out carefully the stone walling, cut it, coat in Copydex and apply to the wall. To finish off the walling, there may be a small gap between the top of the walling and the polystyrene scenery that needs filling. I used polystyrene tile glue to fill in this gap.

The highlight of this layout will be the Faller car system which will give further movement on the layout in the form of working vehicles.

Now for installing the automatic roadway system, also produced by Faller, which is a very ingenious system that allows lorries and buses to move along a thin steel wire placed in the roadway. It also brings a layout to life, as something else, other than the trains, is moving.

Lay down the metal wire using masking tape, then glue down the Faller roadway cards on top, again using Copydex. When laying the return loop accommodated in the hill, make sure that there is enough clearance around the track and that the circle is not too sharp or the vehicles won't be able to negotiate it. Returning now to the town area, lay the wire in the previously marked sheets, making sure you allow for vehicles to slew out round sharp corners. Check that the vehicles move around the circuit correctly, then glue down the roadways. While this system can be expensive, it is worth getting and laying the wires early in construction under the roadway rather than ripping up all your hard work later. You can then buy the vehicles later.

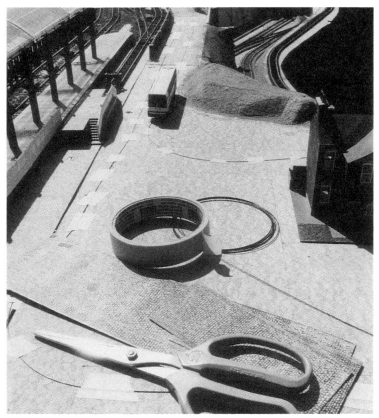

Once the route of the roadway has been decided the 'follow wire' can be taped to the baseboard and tested with a vehicle.

Always look for applications for various mouldings. Here, a Peco N-gauge concrete platform edge has been used as a supporting beam for the road.

Part of the roadway sticks out over the centre tunnel mouth so you need some sort of beam to represent a support. I used two lengths of Peco N-gauge station edging upside down, glued together onto the edge of the Sundeala sub base.

Make up a simple mask when spraying the Langley retaining wall. A dark grey from a mini-spray aerosol.

The retaining wall should also be spray-painted. You can simply do this by using a piece of card cut to shape as a mask, then use a small dark grey mini-spray aerosol to spray paint it. Be careful of overspray.

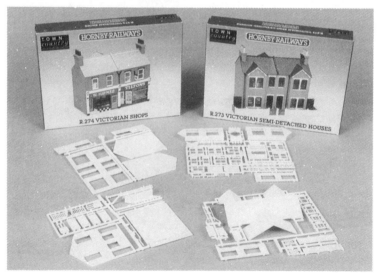

Hornby Railways offer two excellent period buildings ideally suited to this layout. R274 Victorian shops and R273 Victorian semi-detached houses.

These are the semi-detached houses built up and painted by my good friend, Alan Maynard. Several can and have been stuck together as will be seen later.

I dealt with scenic boundaries such as fences and walling in Chapter 12. The houses and shops used for the town are also available from Hornby. They are injection moulded kits that make up into good representations of Victorian buildings, and they are well detailed. You can carry out simple conversions to give varied formations. Again, the final painting, given care and patience, will result in very attractive models. They are complete with gutters, doors, curtains, front walling and basic interior walls and stairs.

Now add other details to the layout; these include telegraph poles, lineside huts, and signals. As I said earlier, it's the details that make for realism.

The main wall around the perimeter of the upper level mainline station is made from a Wills retaining wall kit. Cut two strips of walling from each of the walling sheets about 32mm deep in 4mm scale, ie. 8ft high in real life. Glue the two pieces together as a sandwich, add the buttress pieces either side at one end only, then the top stones along the length and the cap stone on top of the buttress. Then glue sections in place, both together using polystyrene glue and to the baseboard with UHU. Later, paint and, again, lightly weather it.

I always like to finish the edge off around the front and sides of the layout with thin plywood shaped to the contours of the baseboard. Nice flowing lines at the front make a model railway set-up more attractive to the eye and should put you in good favour with the household management!

Building the retaining wall around the station and loco shed area. Using Wills embossed sheets and top caps, construction is simple.

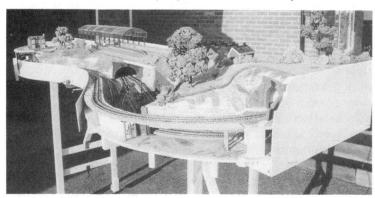

Finishing off the layout is important for good presentation. Some of the thin ply is being persuaded to follow the front profiled baseboard.

With the ply surrounds fitted and the controls finished off, the layout becomes very presentable. Don't forget a track diagram with all the points numbered corresponding to the switches for the first time guest operators — there'll be many, I'm sure.

So what initially started off as a 'big boy' playing with toy trains will actually end up as a set that can be the focal point of the living room etc. It is something that can be shown off to visitors and friends but, more importantly, it makes and creates talking points of interest. It is, in fact, a sort of 3D picture.

14 STOCK

Star for me in the locomotive department is this excellent model of a Britannia class 4-6-2 loco 'William Shakespeare' from Hornby.

I decided from the outset that my version of this layout will be the British Rail period when steam was still dominant. Locos were cleanish and the diesels of the green period were starting to come in. However, it doesn't really matter what anyone else thinks; run whatever stock takes your fancy – after all it's your model railway!

The layout design with its hidden storage sidings will allow four complete trains to be stored, then a further train can be held in the terminus station platform. Furthermore, I decided that several trains from different regions would be seen together with one set of coaches served by two locos. This will result in an excess of motive power which can be held in the running shed on the upper level.

Midland Pullman emerges from the tunnel on the lower circuit. In the foreground is the line up to the terminus. In the background an A4 awaits its turn, while the 0-6-0 Jinty is prepared for 'banking' duties. Just some of the operational scope.

The siding below the retaining wall is there to hold a goods train (probably coal) that can do circuits round the lower level then set back into the siding. The other small siding can be used in two ways. The first is to hold a tank engine 'banker', say a Jinty 0-6-0, that can assist a train up the incline to the terminus once it has gone through the reverse loop. With the tunnel mouth set under the town, when the front of a loco is seen in the mouth, the rear of the train is clear of the main points so it could then set back into one of the empty storage sidings. Secondly, it can be used to hold a mainline loco that has reversed down from the terminus and turned on the reverse loop before it returns to the upper level running shed. This movement eliminates the need for a turntable, which can take up a lot of space, even if it is impressive.

There are two isolation sections of track at the end of the two terminus roads complete with uncoupling ramps, so, as the train enters the terminus, it stops, uncouples and then it can be isolated. Once the train departs, the loco can then be turned on the reverse lower loop and returned to the loco shed.

Suggested stock so far includes an A4 Mallard with three Gresley coaches in blood and custard livery. Then there is a blood and custard rake of MK1 coaches with a Britannia and 2-10-0 9F locomotives. One of my favourites, perhaps a little out of period, is the maroon Coronation Scot streamlined 4-6-2 with period LMS rake.

The platforms will accommodate a rake of three coaches and two locos. The *pièce de résistance* for me is the old Tri-ang Midland Blue Pullman train. This is a four car set, two power units and two centre or parlor cars.

Other locos in the Hornby range include 8F 2-8-0, Hunt class 4-4-0, 4-6-2 A3, 4-6-2 Coronation Scot, 0-4-0 Saddle tank and 0-4-0 diesel shunter.

Locos from the Replica range include 4-6-0 B1, 0-6-0 Collett, 0-6-0 Pannier tank and 0-6-0 03.

From Dapol we have an Austerity 0-6-0, 0-6-0 Terrier, 4-6-0 County and class 56 diesel.

Lima have the biggest range of diesel traction models which include 08, class 47 (× 2), class 37, class 40 and class 87 electric.

With so much in the way of stock available, it can be very difficult to make a decision on what sort of stock to run and what period to model. I include some selections of locos that are available from the major ready-to-run manufacturers. These include Hornby, Lima, Dapol, Replica and Bachmann. I haven't included rolling-stock, as there would not be enough space.

Finally, bringing things bang up-to-date, is the Hornby Railways class 91 for the East Coast main line.

Because of the large plastic frogs on the Hornby points, the locos can sometimes stutter. This is due to the system used for electrical pick-up on the locos and tenders. Today's Hornby locos are wired in such a way that the tender picks up from one rail, the loco from the other, thus giving the two polarities needed to power the motor. So, to help solve this problem we can add extra pick-ups to the loco and tender. The more wheels you pick up from, the better the running will be, especially through the points and, as a bonus, the slow running will improve. The Tasmar high frequency track cleaning unit will help in the general running, as it combats surface dirt on the track. It breaks it down through high frequency power.

As a model is taken out of the box, it is bright, shiny and not too authentic, so a bit of careful weathering is needed to bring the loco to life. Again, it is not easy to show this in black and white, so I can only advise that you look at old colour photos in some of the many full-size oriented magazines and books. Be careful, though, that the subject chosen is not a preserved item that has been lovingly restored to pristine condition rather like the one you've just taken out of the box – this is not authentic steam period condition.

In general, two basic colours are adequate for weathering if they are applied in different strengths. By this, I mean how much thinner has been added to the base colour, so that, when it is sprayed, it doesn't swamp the detail. Washes of black can be applied with a brush around the smokebox, footplate, boiler top and cab roof; anywhere, in fact, that soot and dust are likely to settle. Rust colour should be applied to the lower mechanisms, such as valve gear, wheels, brakes and axleboxes on the tender. Also highlight in silver areas that are worn such as steps and handrails. The latter are best dry brushed, and this technique can also be used to highlight detail such as rivets, pipes etc in their respective colours.

To dry brush, take a brush and cover it with paint, then wipe it dry on a suitable cloth or tissue until almost dry, then carefully flick the bristles across the detail. Paint will be deposited on this detail only, thus highlighting it. The degree of highlighting is determined by how much paint is applied, ie. the number of coats.

Another area where a degree of individualism can be achieved is by adding further details to your locos and, of course, stock. Details such as lamps, crew, vacuum pipes, brakes where required, tools such as shovels, and oil cans, in fact all the sort of items usually seen on a loco; again, study photos.

To take detailing one stage further, Crownline from Cornwall offer an enormous range of detailing kits suitable for a very wide range of ready-to-run locos. They range from simple detailing kits to almost complete rebuilds into a different class.

This type of kit will start you on the road to real modelling, then conversions, simple kits in white metal, and onto etched brass until you take on the challenge of scratch building.

15 MODELLING TIPS

In order to operate a successful model railway, some basic areas need attention from time to time. Like any large machine, a good oiling now and then keeps it moving, but don't overdo it.

Cleanliness is the key word to running successfully a model railway. I emphasize 'running', as it is very easy to obtain a large static layout and is so hard to maintain even a smallish, fully-working layout. Both track and locos should be cleaned regularly.

After solder, and in particular flux, has come into contact with the track, ie. the soldered electrical connections, always make sure that there are no soldered areas on the rail. If so, file them down, but be careful not to damage the rail surface, otherwise rusting/corrosion may set in at a later date. Clean the track thoroughly with a suitable abrasive rubber, available from Fleischmann or Peco.

Maintenance of locos and track is important. Liquid cleaner from Herkat using a dust-free rag and a rubber style track cleaner from Fleischmann.

Where glue from the scenic application may have spilt onto the rail surface, the rubber will show it up. Those areas should be chipped off with a knife and then cleaned with the rubber. Subsequent cleaning can be undertaken using methylated spirits or an excellent all-purpose cleaner called Modelbahnol SR24 by Herkat. Using this cleaner regularly will eliminate excessive use of the abrasive track cleaner. Apply the liquid cleaner with a rag, preferably fluff-free, or a track cleaning car or loco.

You should also clean loco wheels at regular intervals, scraping off any stubborn dirt with a small screwdriver then using a glass fibre pen (as used in cleaning electrical circuit boards). Stock should only need occasional cleaning.

Application of oil to loco axles, motors, gears etc. should be very sparing. Don't allow any moving parts to go dry, so keep them lightly oiled. Also remove any fluff or dirt that may have accumulated around the moving parts, such as axles, wheels etc.

I have mentioned soldering electrical joints. This subject holds many fears for a lot of modellers. There are basically two different temperatures of soldering applied to different materials. These are normal 4-core soldering and, more specialized but very relevant to model railways, white metal soldering. Both require the same basic technique. The correct soldering iron is essential for the right job. I would recommend an Orynx iron for 4-core soldering, both the 45 watt and 60 watt in their range are ideal. I work on the basis of getting heat into the job allowing the solder to flow and getting the iron out.

Cleanliness is the key word in soldering and a good flux is equally important. Both items being soldered together must be clean. Flux them both liberally, then bring the soldering iron loaded with solder to the joint; the solder will flow easily, after which quickly remove the iron. The joint is almost instant. In the same way, you can separate the items by first fluxing and then re-introducing the soldering iron.

When dealing with white metal, you need a special low temperature controlled iron. The one I would thoroughly recommend, from personal use, is available from Litesold.

While on the subject of fixing things together, we must take a look at gluing. There is a vast array of glues on the market to do any amount of jobs. All I can do is list the ones I use and the applications for which I use them. The most universal is UHU, a multi-use glue for many applications. Be careful when applying it, as it is stringy, so when applying make sure the stringing doesn't go everywhere. On the layout, I used it to stick the tunnel mouths to the board, and plastic walls to the base, indeed anytime that two unlike materials need to be joined. It is ideal for metal, wood, glass etc. For joining like materials, I use Evostick Resin W wood glue for wood; Copydex for gluing cardboard to several different materials such as wood and even polystyrene tiles. Polystyrene tiles are glued together with polystyrene tile glue available from Texas Homecare. And then there is super-glue. There are now so many various types and makes on the market to do every conceivable job, that it is difficult to know which is the best. The one I use, again only a personal preference, is by Loctite, because it comes in a very practical single drop dispenser tube, which means it lasts longer before it clogs up. Superglue will shatter if the items joined together are dropped. Finally, there are two part epoxy resin glues, of which there are several available.

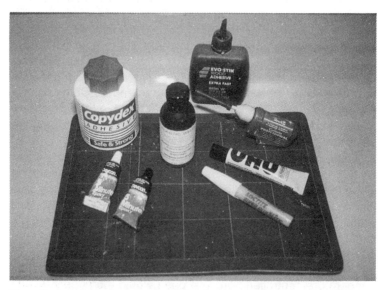

It's quite surprising how many different glues were used during the construction of this layout. Featured here are 5-min 2-part epoxy resin, superglue, UHU, Revel plastic glue, Plastic Weld, Copydex and Evo-stik Resin W.

When using any glues, where only a small amount is required on a joint, then squeeze out or mix-up a small sample on a scrap piece of card or wood and then, using a cocktail stick, apply sparingly a small amount of glue to the required joint.

Whether you are gluing or soldering, holding the items to be joined together is another key factor to a successful joint. For example, when gluing two pieces of wood together once the glue has been applied and the pieces of wood joined, place a suitable clamp around it and, within minutes, the joint will be strong, although it is best to leave it overnight, or better still 24 hours to really harden off.

Apart from the superglues where the joint is almost instant, most glues take time to cure, generally 24 hours. There are many clamps available to do most jobs, and some you will have to adapt yourself to do awkward jobs.

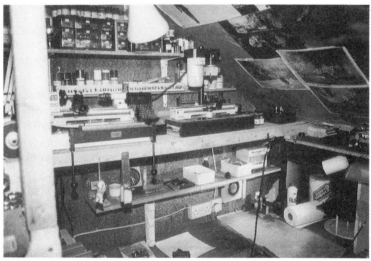

A workshop such as this takes many years to build up and, while all this isn't required from the outset, it makes life easier later on.

When undertaking modelling, you don't have to own a complete workshop; a range of simple tools is all that is needed to make a start. I mentioned at the beginning of the book the basic tools required for woodwork. For modelling, the list is also fairly small, although my range of tools has grown over the years as I've acquired more sophisticated tools to help do the simple jobs in a better and more accurate fashion. Here I'm referring to such things as a lathe and milling machine. While they weren't essential in the beginning, they have now become to me another right arm.

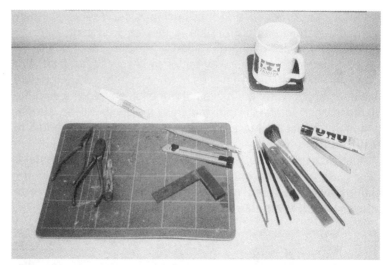

Basic tools needed for a basic workbench: cutting mat, square, knife, pencil, screwdriver, cutters, pliers, two files, three different-sized paint brushes, 6-inch steel ruler, scriber, fibre pen, UHU and superglue.

A firm base on which to work is always preferable. I have a piece of plate glass on top of a suitable desk. Choose a comfortable working height and, most important, a comfortable chair. Next is a cutting mat. This allows the knife to cut through the material you're cutting and into the mat, but won't blunt the blade as easily as if you were directly cutting onto a hard surface. The knife I use is one by Edding and has blades that can be snapped off. There are five new edges per refill, a lot easier than unscrewing the handle and fitting a new blade when you're right in the middle of a cut.

When cutting, a straight edge is important, so a good metal ruler is useful – 6 inches long is adequate, 12 inches ideal. Also most definitely required is a 4-inch engineer's square. In this hobby, anything not square stands out like a sore thumb, so get it right from the start.

You require a decent HB pencil and a metal scriber, along with a couple of Swiss files (here I use a rats-tail and a fine grade triangular) and several different paint brushes. Tweezers are a must, as are a fibre glass pen with refills and an electric drill with accessories. It is this last item that has the most uses when used with a range of various attachments. Black and Decker market the Minicraft range of tools, ideally suited to the modeller. A Buffalo electric hand drill with a variable speed transformer is a lifetime's investment. Useful attachments that I would recommend are a circular saw, a slitting disc and diamond impregnated rubber wheel all on their own arbours, plus a number of routers and a good set of numbered drills.

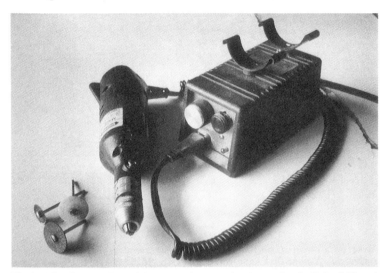

Black & Decker market 'right arms' here in the form of a Buffalo drill and variable speed controller, plus cutters, routers, etc., in their Minicraft range.

The three main attachments mentioned are ideal for the following purposes: the circular saw will cut plastics, wood etc; the slitting disc will cut through any metal section, particularly rail (ideal for isolation gaps); the rubber wheel is excellent for removing solder from brass and routers to machine away plastic, white metal etc. As you can see this is a very useful and important addition to the modelling workshop.

Finally, you need several types of glue, eg. UHU, superglue and two part epoxy. You won't be able to get them all at once, but get maybe one or two each time you visit an exhibition or model shop.

Finally, take care of your tools and they'll last. Before filing, run the serrations through talcum powder to stop metal clogging the cutting surface, and make up a useful stand for the flux bottle and drill bits. Keep the soldering iron tips clean by wiping dirt from them with a rag, and then re-tin them each time. As this is done when the iron's on, *be careful*.

When drilling a hole, start with a small drill first as a pilot, then step up in drill size to the actual size for the hole you require.

Don't make a drill chatter or do too much work – you'll shorten its life by blunting it.

Make up a small stand to house the drill bits and bottle of flux used in soldering. It's much easier when tools are to hand. Also pictured is a soldering iron from Orynx.

When cutting, draw the knife across the line lightly first, holding it close against your metal edge, then increase the pressure slowly on each successive pass until you make a complete cut. When gluing, do it sparingly; build up in small amounts, rather than a sudden rush from the tube (when you press too hard) that runs everywhere and ruins the job. Keep your working surface clean. Give yourself room with the various parts laid out in sequences of construction.

16 GETTING NEARER THE PROTOTYPE

At the beginning of this book, I said that I would concentrate on building this particular layout I've designed, and build it using examples from the very extensive Hornby model railways range. So to conclude this book I ask the question 'where do you go after this project is completed?'

There are nearly as many kinds of model railways as there are railway modellers so, before designing the layout, think about what you want from it. Is your chief interest in operation, scenery, or loco building? Do you prefer the main line, branch line or light-railway scene; the activity of a station or the occasionally broken peace of a line between stations? Or do you simply need a test track where your latest loco can be put through its paces?

Fine scale modelling is something that takes time and experience to achieve. A shot of my second layout called 'Bevet', which is a small modular style layout. Here an 0-6-0ST Special Tank is being coaled up and watered.

The main line scene requires either a smaller scale or more obvious compression of the length of trains and the size of stations. If your preference is for this type of railway, are you prepared for the extra space, extra work or compromises that this will involve?

Any model railway that is more than just a test-track needs a convincing and coherent 'story' behind it. This means that the builder must have thought about where the line is supposed to be situated; why it was built (for example to carry coal from mines to a seaport or to bring farm produce into a developing township); and when the period illustrated by the model is supposed to be. The answers to any or all of these questions may come from the desire to include a favourite loco, item of rolling-stock or style of architecture.

There is immense scope for ideas in this area of layout planning. One can model a line which actually exists, or has existed, finding out from published histories or local records how the place looked in the chosen period. One can place an imaginary line, either independent or owned by one of the 'big four', in a real location, but make sure there is a real reason for the railway being there. One can model part of a real company in an imaginary location, so the line and history can all be totally freelance. Some very fine layouts have been built by modellers who invented not only the railway but the town and even the entire country in which it was located!

The important thing is that the railway should be consistent within itself and with its surroundings. If you think this all too pedantic, it is only necessary to visit a few model railway exhibitions and look at the different types of layouts on show; those that really 'come across' and involve the spectator are those where all the above questions have been fully thought out and answered.

Also to be considered in choosing a theme is the prototype – the original 12in to the foot from which model railways originate. The setting for the layout can be based on a real location or it can be totally fictitious; it can be set in this country or abroad; it can be built to portray any particular historical period (bearing in mind that it would look a bit odd if one were to see an Inter City 125 roaring past a background of the Battle of Hastings!). This is where the modeller's imagination can really be let loose. Many modellers approach this in the same way as a painter creating a scene on canvas, but in this medium, it is three-dimensional.

Being a modular layout, Bevet is made up of several scenes. We saw the country section earlier; here is the Victorian seaside scene complete with over one hundred hand-painted Prieser figures.

Both layouts mentioned, Bevet and Bevleys, were built to P4 (18.83 track gauge) standards and are based on LNWR practice at the turn of the century.

Remember, once you begin to scenic a layout, you're no longer 'playing with a train set', you're building a model railway.

The next step is to decide upon a region. In the UK, the main railway grid is run by British Rail, although there are also various tourist railways, industrial railways and a few metropolitan lines. The history of the railway in Britain is long and complex and would fill a fair-sized bookshelf, but a basic understanding will help enormously in your choice of region. Up until 1923, there were over a hundred independently owned railways throughout Britain. In 1923, Parliament engineered a reorganization, merging all of them into four large companies known as the 'big four'. These were the London Midland and Scottish Railway (LMS or LMSR), the London and North Eastern Railway (LNER), the Great Western Railway (GWR) and the Southern Railway (SR). In 1948, they were nationalized and came under the banner of British Railways, evolving in 1964 into British Rail. Out of the original 'big four' only the GWR managed to retain its own identity, in that most of its stock remained very much the same after the nationalization. Individual and distinctive liveries stayed the same and it is mainly for this reason that more GWR models are available from the trade.

Having chosen a theme and a region, you might like to think about joining a model railway society. There are many of these around the country.

You may also consider a change of gauge or look at more prototypical-looking stock, etc., within the scale you already model. You may remember that, in our breakdown of scales and gauges at the start of the book within 4mm modelling, there were three track gauges 16.5 (00), 18.2 (EM) and 18.83 (S4). It was the last of these that I chose to model, along with a particular interest in the old 'Premier Line' which was the LNWR.

This near-to-exact scale modelling satisfied the requirement that I needed to get out of the hobby and I include a few photos of my two exhibition layouts 'Bevleys' and 'Bevet' that, between them, have attended over 50 exhibitions up and down the country. Now this really is a reward for all your hard work and certainly can be considered the icing on the cake.

As a member of a club where experience, advice and encouragement will usually be showered upon you, you can gain the opportunity to exhibit your work. . .go on, have a go!

17 INSTANT MODEL RAILWAY

I have deliberately kept the construction of this layout and the products used as simple as possible. As Hornby model railway products are easily obtainable worldwide, I've purposely stuck with their products for this layout and book. I could easily fill another volume of similar size to this one with alternative products to those used.

Lima's excellent instant model railway gives an ideal base to start from. There is plenty of scope to add further scenic material such as trees, hedges etc., plus various weathering as required.

For those who are still a bit hesitant to have a go, there are on the market today a number of ready-built, instant layouts. This type of thing has been available to European modellers for a number of years, from such manufacturers as Noch and Faller in several gauges. Lima, based in Italy, have also had these styles of layouts for a while. They have, however, only been available in England for a short period of time.

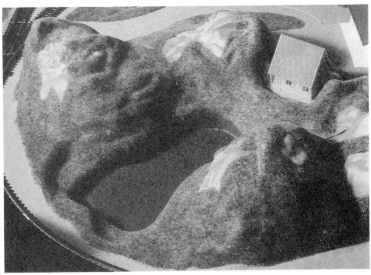

Inside the hill is a small lake. The hill is covered in grass, but really needs some trees, fences and bushes to complete it.

You can pay a fair amount of money for different-sized sets and details. I have chosen to look at one priced at just under £100. It consists of track already pinned/or glued down, houses in place, and all this on a strong plastic base that has had a degree of scenic material and paint applied. Also included is a transformer/controller that just needs connecting up and plugging in, plus, of course, there is the train. All you need to start instantly operating a model railway.

These sets are an ideal way to gain confidence, as they will still need a degree of detailing and weathering. For example, that bright shiny rail is crying out for a coat of rust paint. Hedges, houses, trees and additional layers of scenic flocks can be added to the existing covering. A wooden frame can also be construct-ed to go under the plastic base which can include legs, etc. And, of course, the stock can be weathered.

For reasons of simplicity, I've concentrated on one period and looked at one set of stock in 00/H0 gauge. All of the foregoing material can be applied just as easily to other scales and gauges, as well as European- and American-style stock prototypes.

With the amount of stock and material available on the market now, the avid modeller is only really limited by his or her imagination.

18 THE COMPLETED RAILWAY SYSTEM

Above: inside the overall roof with the camera resting on the hydraulic buffer stops. *William Shakespeare*, a 4-6-2 Britannia class loco, is entering the terminus. *Below:* outside in the station forecourt are the waiting double decker buses – one from EFE, and the other a kit-built example.

Above: more kit vehicles are seen on the road running alongside the station and headshunt road to the loco shed. Underneath this road is the wire for the Faller automatic road system. *Below:* where the road crosses over the return loop lines you can see the Peco N-gauge concrete platform edge used as a bridge section. A mixture of scenic materials brings the scene to life.

APPENDIX A
MANUFACTURERS' AND SUPPLIERS' ADDRESSES
(listed in alphabetical order)

UK

Argus Plans
Argus House
Boundary Way
Hemel Hempstead
Hertfordshire
HP2 7ST
Tel: 0442 66551

Carr's Modelling Products
Unit 5. Centre 88
Elm Grove
London
SW19 4HE

Crownline Models
8 Rame Terrace
Rame Cross
Nr Penryn
Cornwall
TR10 9DZ

Hornby Model Railways
Westwood
Margate
Kent
CT9 4JX

Lima Model Railways
Riko International
Hemel Hempstead
Hertfordshire

Litesold (soldering irons)
97-99 Gloucester Road
Croydon
CR0 2DN

Model Images Retail
(also Mail Order)
56 Station Road
Letchworth
Hertfordshire
SG6 3BE
Tel. 0462 684859

Model Masters (Trees)
50a Clifton Road
Weston-Super-Mare
Avon
BS23 1BW
Tel. 0934 629717

Models and Railways
(Importers of Faller, Preiser figures,
Fleischmann track rubber)
Unit 8
Mill Road
Brighton
West Sussex

Orynx (soldering irons)
Portman Road
Reading
Berkshire
RG3 1NE
Tel. 0734 595843

Peco
Beer
Seaton
Devon
EX12 3NA

Replica Railways
Station Yard
Station Road
Lambourn
Berkshire
RG16 7PH

Tasmar Products
31 Kneesworth Street
Royston
Hertfordshire
SG8 5AB

W & H (Models) Ltd
(Importers of Marklin)
14 New Cavendish Street
London W1

USA

Euro-Rails Model Importers Ltd
465 McCall Road
Rochester
NY 14616
Tel: (716) 663 1160

Wm K Walthers
5601 Florist Avenue
Milwaukee
WI 53218

APPENDIX B GLOSSARY

abutment	lateral support at the end of an arch or bridge.
adhesion	contact between wheel and rail.
ballast	material placed between sleepers.
banking	assisting a train ascending a gradient by attaching one or more locos at the rear.
bay platform	short terminal platform let into a longer one.
bogie	short wheelbase truck with four or six wheels which can pivot at the centre at which it is attached to the underframe of a loco or other vehicle.
cab control	operating one or more model trains singly or simultaneously.
cant	amount by which one rail of a curved track is raised above the other.
catenary	supporting cable for conductive wire of an overhead electrification system.
coupling	device for connecting vehicles together.
diagram	display of trackwork and signals controlled by a signalbox.
distant signal	signal warning approaching trains of the state of stop signals ahead.
end-to-end	layout with a terminal at either end.
fiddle yard	set of sidings where trains are terminated and stored.
fishplates	metal or plastic (insulated) plates for joining rail lengths together.

flange	inside projecting edge of a wheel.
freelance	a model not directly based on an actual prototype.
frogs	centre crossing vee of a point which can be 'insulated', made out of plastic or 'live' using metal rail. Live frogs give better running.
gauge	distance between rails of a track.
gradient grade	slope or inclination to the horizontal.
halt	stopping place without station facilities for local lines.
headshunt	road running parallel with the main line for shunting.
home signal	semaphore stop signal.
hump yard	marshalling yard with artificial mound for the purpose of gravity wagon sorting.
inspection saloon	Chief Medical Engineer's private coach.
island platform	platform with tracks on both sides.
key	wedge of wood or steel holding rail in the chair bolted to the sleeper in position at the correct gauge.
level crossing	where two railways or a road and railway cross at the same level.
light engine	locomotive without train.
limit of shunt	board marking the limit of the shunt area.
loading gauge	the limiting height and width of rolling stock and loads to ensure adequate lineside clearance.
loop	continuous circular connection between up and down lines.
marshalling yard	place where wagons are sorted and assembled into trains.
motor bogies	bogie with driving wheels or motorized axles.
multiple track	section of track with more than one up and one down line.
multiple unit	a 'set' of coaches internally powered by diesel or electric motors, operated by one driver.

narrow gauge	railway track of less then the standard gauge of 4ft 8½in.
packing	maintaining the correct sleeper level by adjusting the ballast.
pantagraph	link between overhead catenary system and the train or loco.
permanent way	track bed and tracks in position.
pilot	extra loco coupled to the front end of the train loco to give extra power over steep gradients.
platelayer	track maintenance man.
point	place at which trains can be directed onto another line.
pullman car	railway carriage providing high standard of comfort and service.
rail car	self-propelled passenger-carrying vehicle.
rolling-stock	carriages and wagons.
scenic break	a block in a layout to separate differing scenic backgrounds.
semaphore	type of signal with a pivoted arm which can be raised or lowered.
siding	line used for temporary accommodation of vehicles.
starter signal	signal giving authority to a train to proceed.
shunt	to move vehicles onto a minor track, to marshal vehicles into a particular order.
shuttle	regular return service over a short route.
six-footway	area between parallel tracks.
sleeper	beam for holding rails to correct gauge.
solebar	main frame part of wagon underframe.
standard gauge	4ft 8½in between rails.
tank locomotive	loco which carries coal and water supplies on its own main frames.
tank wagon	freight vehicle built to carry liquid or gas in a tank-like container.
tender locomotive	loco which carries its coal supplies in a separate permanently-coupled vehicle called a tender.

terminal	end of the line or departure point, including station, switches, buildings and other equipment.
tail lamp	lamp located at the rear of the last vehicle.
turntable	a rotating mechanism which turns locos around.
underbridge	underline bridge carrying train over road, river etc.
underframe	framework under the body of a carriage.

INDEX

Adjustable foot 47

Ballast 50, 51, 53
Banker 99
Baseboard 12, 40
Big four 115
Buildings 94, 95

Chipboard 12
Crownline 103

Dapol 101
Droppers 69

Electric points 54, 60, 61, 62
Expanded polystyrene 76, 77

Faller roadway 71, 72, 92, 93
Farish, Graham 21
Folding stays 39
Framework 36
Frogs 66, 67, 102, 124

Gauges 15
   0 17
   00/H0 17
   1 16
   EM 17
   N 18
   S 19
   Scalefour (S4) 17
   TT 18
   Z 18
Glues 53, 106

Hornby 100
Hydraulic buffer stops 54
Incline piers 55, 56, 78

Insulated fishplates 57

Layout design 25
Legs 39
Lima 101, 116

Mighty Mallard set 22
Minicraft 109

Plans Services 28, 121
Plastic Weld 89

Replica 100
Retaining wall 74, 75, 94, 96
Reverse curve 26, 61

Scale 15
Shrubs 83
Soldering irons 110
Station 88
Sundeala 12

Tasma controller 45, 59
Tools
   modelling 108
   track-pinning 49
   woodworking 33
Trees 85
Track
   cleaner 58, 63, 104
   components 29
   diagram 30
Tunnel mouths 73, 87

Underlay 50, 52

Video 79, 80

Wood measurements 28

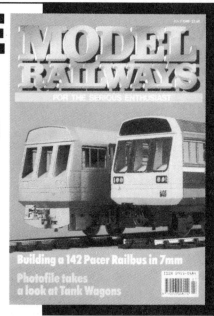
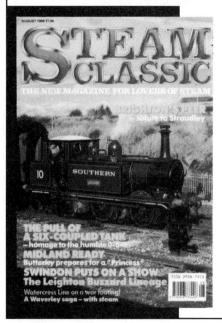